ORNAMENTAL
Vegetable Gardening

Sally Gregson

THE CROWOOD PRESS

First published in 2009 by
The Crowood Press Ltd
Ramsbury, Marlborough
Wiltshire SN8 2HR

www.crowood.com

British Library Cataloguing-in-Publication Data

A catalogue record for this book is available from the British Library.

ISBN 978 1 84797 117 3

Dedication
For Henry Heard

Typeset by Florence Production Ltd, Stoodleigh, Devon

Printed and bound in Malaysia by Times Offset (M) Sdn Bhd

Contents

Acknowledgements

I have had lots of encouragement and active help during the process of writing this book. Above all from my long-suffering, vegetable-gardening husband, Peter, who has given me his unstinting support throughout. In particular, he has read through the proofs and corrected my mistakes, for which I am very grateful.

In addition, I would like to thank the owners of the beautiful gardens that I have written about and photographed in this book: Sarah Mead and Head Gardener, James Cox, of Holt Farm, Somerset; Frances Young of Stoberry, Wells; Roy and Helen Stickland, Julia Grace, Shane Allen, Julia Thyer, John Beauchamp and Adrian Hutchinson. And my thanks to the Royal Horticultural Society for allowing me to photograph their potager and ornamental vegetable garden at Rosemoor, Devon, and to Aberglasny Restoration Trust, Carmarthenshire, Wales.

I am also indebted to Rowan Isaac for the cover image of The Old Vicarage, Maisiemore, Gloucester; and to Adrian Hutchinson for his images of the Château of Villandry, France.

Introduction

Vegetable gardening has always been a popular and rewarding pastime ever since peas and beans were grown in cottage gardens; the wartime 'Dig for Victory' campaigns; and the self-sufficiency movement of the 1970s 'good-lifers'. Now in the twenty-first century a whole new generation of gardeners is bringing an altogether different approach to 'growing their own'.

Where once leeks and parsnips were grown 'super-sized' for exhibition, now we like to pick them small and sweet for the kitchen. Where once gardeners were impelled to use every poisonous pesticide available to eliminate all insect life, now we want to know just what chemicals, if any, have been sprayed on our food. Where supermarkets once were proud to fly in 'fresh' produce from all over the world, now we are concerned about 'food miles' and the future of our precious green planet. And where once the economics of buying seed and 'growing your own' did not square up to low supermarket prices, now in our present more straitened circumstances, home-grown produce makes better sense. And the reward is that inimitable flavour of vegetables picked, prepared and eaten within an hour or two.

So perhaps it's time for vegetable growing to throw off its cloth cap and muddy wellies image, come out from behind the garden fence and proudly take centre stage. For, no matter how small the garden or how short our spare time is, if we can create a vegetable garden that is as beautiful to look at as it is productive, healthy and economic, it will have earned its days in the sun.

It may be formally laid out with symmetrical beds that impart their own satisfying sense of order. It may be big enough to include annual flowers grown both for decoration and as pest deterrents.

Or it may be confined to a few big pots on a terrace or balcony, filled with special salad mixes ready at hand for the kitchen.

Whatever the design, by dividing up the growing area into manageable parts, each will be easier and quicker to deal with individually than one large plot that is always crying out for attention. Each small area takes a shorter time to tend, fitting in with a busy family life more easily. And growing fewer

Strawberries, salads and herbs in a terracotta pot.

plants of each variety avoids those gluts. Fresh vegetables eaten in season taste so much better than frozen bags of insipid summer surpluses. Smaller quantities of seed can be sown little and often to achieve a succession of crops over a longer period. And fast-growing salads can be squeezed alongside slower crops that take up to a year to mature.

This book features real ornamental gardens, both large and small, ranging from the elaborate parterre at the Château of Villandry in the Loire Valley bedded out with rows of ornamental cabbages and lettuces, romantic rose-covered arbours and burbling dipping-pools, to organic potagers supplying the needs of a growing young family, and smaller areas catering simply for two people who care about what they eat. The principles and process of designing, laying out, preparing the beds and planting are explained in detail. Some of the actual garden plans are reproduced, and work in progress is pictured.

In all, the aim is to demystify growing vegetables. There is a lot of hokum put about by those old gardeners with mud on their wellies. Vegetable seed germinates easily. If it fails to do so, it's often the weather conditions that are quirky. Each year, the weather pattern is unique. Some years are good for some vegetables and bad for others. Successes and failures make philosophers of all gardeners. A calendar of when to sow, transplant and harvest is at the end of the book (*see* Appendix). It's there as a guide, not a rulebook.

Breeding work is being carried out all the time. Work is being done to develop varieties that cope successfully with Britain's cool, damp climate when they might naturally be more at home on the shores of the Mediterranean or in Peru. Many traditional vegetables are being bred to improve disease resistance and even to be unpalatable to pests, thereby obviating the need to spray. These varieties are recommended and listed individually in Chapter 8, as are the most decorative forms of lettuce, kale and cabbage, for example.

The easy way to grow each vegetable is described in detail. Labour-intensive varieties have been left out: celery that needs blanching; celeriac that rarely makes bulbs larger than a golf ball; and winter lettuce that, without fortnightly fungicides, succumbs to mildew.

But not all vegetables are decorative. Some are dull and green, but delicious family favourites. So what better way to bring a bit of colour than to grow annual flowers alongside them? Some flowers, such as French marigolds (*Tagetes*), attract beneficial insects such as hoverflies. These voracious little chaps are born and brought up to eat greenfly and blackfly for breakfast, lunch and tea. Flowers that attract aphids are also named and shamed. Pot marigolds (*Calendula*), for instance, are very orange and pretty, but they host blackfly.

Some flowers for cutting, such as dahlias and gladioli, and those for drying, such as sea lavenders and straw flowers, are better suited to growing among the vegetables in rows, so that they can be picked for the house. They need more attention than they get in the wider garden. Sweet peas are lovely scrambling through the herbaceous border, but for cutting they need to be grown up supports and picked daily.

Some flowers are good to eat too. The little flowers of heartsease (*Viola tricolor*) and blue borage (*Borago officinalis*) are pretty, as well as being delicious sprinkled over a salad. Sunflowers are fun and easy to grow, especially for young apprentices. Their dried seeds can also be stored to sprinkle over breakfast cereals, or toasted and scattered over a winter salad. They are all included in a list of flowers and herbs to grow alongside the vegetables (*see* Chapter 9).

So, very soon – within just a few months – not only will the garden be a pleasure to work in, but there will be delicious vegetables and flowers to eat young, sweet and fresh. And if you discount your time, you will have saved on the supermarket bills and even, perhaps, the season ticket to the gym!

Flowers for cutting and drying.

CHAPTER 1

A potted history

Old walled gardens are magical places. Push open the gate and the spirit of a once-bustling kitchen garden is almost tangible. Less than a century ago men and boys would have been planting, hoeing and harvesting neat rows of vegetables and fruit. In the temperate houses, the Head Gardener might have been meticulously pruning the figs, grapes and peaches. And in the hothouses rows of exotic pot plants would have been waiting their turn to decorate the grand house. It all seems just out of sight, just beyond recall, a faint breath of another age evaporated in the sun.

Seventeenth-century gardeners' labyrinth.

Such gardens were an integral part of every wealthy Victorian country house and surprisingly of more modest houses too. They were a status symbol. And, well run, they were essential to the everyday lives of the owners, their visitors and weekend guests and of course to their numerous servants.

The Head Gardener was responsible for provisioning the kitchens with the choicest vegetables and fruit in, or out of, season for his employers and for providing more humble fare for his fellow staff. Flowers were picked for the dining table, sometimes to match the hostess's dress. Huge arrangements were constructed by the Housekeeper on the grand table in the hall. Palms, aspidistras and ferns were grown in the conservatory where tea was taken on rainy days. And bedding plants for the borders around the house were raised, planted, weeded and replenished throughout the year. The whole enterprise depended on the knowledge and experience of the Head Gardener and the skill of his team, while its economics relied on the huge variation of wealth between the owners and their staff.

All this more or less ended with the outbreak of the First World War. Some walled gardens survived the period between the wars, but by the end of the Second World War society had changed for ever. The grandsons of those Victorian gardeners expected higher wages and better living conditions. The gap between the wealth of the owners and their staff narrowed. Without dozens of staff to run the houses and a large team of gardeners to tend those beautiful gardens, they became an unaffordable anachronism. The weeds overwhelmed them.

But where had those gardens come from? What had preceded them? And why was their layout formal and symmetrical? The answers lie buried in the past, unrecorded, merely implied.

Gardens in the West undoubtedly had their origins in the 'paradise gardens' of ancient Persia and Mesopotamia. It is well documented that the garden, or 'paradise', would have been square and enclosed within a high wall. Paths and watercourses were originally laid out in a cruciform pattern, with a 'Tree of Life' in the centre. Contemporary depictions often show a date palm entwined with four snakes to represent the four winds. The paths or canals of the garden were fixed on the compass points and each quarter represented the four known continents of the world. It was a cool, shaded place; a refuge from the bustle of the street and the heat of the sun. Splashing fountains sparkled and the scents of roses, lilies and jasmine were confined within the walls. Flowers and vegetables were tended in the beds and fruit and vines grown against the walls.

This basic pattern was repeated throughout the ancient world and taken up by the Roman empire. The vineyard at Pompeii is laid out in just this pattern. When the Romans came to Britain they laid out their new gardens and vineyards along the same formal, symmetrical lines. They brought with them all the familiar Mediterranean vegetables and in particular the medicinal herbs that they could not find growing wild in British hedgerows. Thyme, hyssop, rosemary and lavender, to name but a very few, are all natives of southern Europe. Formal beds outlined with box would have contained cucumbers, globe artichokes and figs. There is evidence that our climate was a degree or two warmer than it is now and vines were grown as far north as Yorkshire, while apricots and peaches were grown against the south-facing walls. Paradise was therefore retained.

When the legions were recalled to Rome, many of these gardens must have disappeared. However, much of the Roman knowledge of the uses of medicinal herbs and the formality of the gardens survived with the religious orders. Monasteries were places of refuge for the sick, and communication with the Continent was maintained. Each religious establishment was run then, as it is today, as a collective. Seed of vegetables and fruit was husbanded each year and grown to feed the numerous clergy. The sick would have been treated in their hospitals with medicines made from wild plants, complemented by the Roman herbs. The monks uniquely would have been able to read the ancient herbals stored in the monastery library. They also knew from centuries-old experience that these plants in particular needed the good drainage and warm soil provided by raised beds edged with timber.

Within each monastery was a quiet cloister garden for contemplation and prayer. It was usually square, enclosed by the cloister walls and divided into a cruciform pattern by paths. Often there was a fountain or small pond in the centre. It was, and is, a little bit of paradise.

Following the eleventh-century invasion by the Norman French, many more religious orders were established in Britain, reinforcing and reinvigorating the knowledge and practices of the existing monasteries. New herbs and vegetable varieties would have been introduced and lost ones reintroduced.

An enclosed paradise garden in the Moorish style: the Generalife gardens of the Alhambra, Granada, southern Spain.

Wall-trained fruit trees make a diamond pattern at Aberglasny, South Wales.

The benefits of several centuries of cultivation and selection on the Continent during the earlier Dark Ages would probably have been made available to the gardener monks, although little is documented.

In the following centuries royalty and the land-owning noblemen would have been growing fruit and vegetables in gardens on their estates, as well as importing them from France. Many of these gardens were enclosed within wattle fences, or hedges. Sometimes the hedges themselves were composed of hazels, gooseberries, currants and blackberries, mingled with thorns, crab apples and medlars in order to be fruitful as well as protective. With the rise of the wealthier 'middle classes', hedges and fences gave way to walls. Apricots, peaches, plums and nectarines were trained against them, interspaced at intervals by standard cherries whose branches were fanned out to shelter the other fruit. Strawberries and flowers were grown in beds beneath dwarf fruit trees. And all was symmetry and formality.

In the sixteenth and seventeenth centuries the explorers and subsequent settlers of the New World brought back increasing numbers of American delicacies, including pumpkins, tomatoes, beans and of course the potato. Vegetable gardens remained enclosed within walls and the beds were still raised by about 15cm (6in) above the level of the ground, but not necessarily in a formal pattern like a parterre.

Many gardens had pavilions or arbours entwined with vines, or sometimes trained apple trees. Some were built of stone and used for storing fruit and dried peas and beans, and some more elaborate pavilions even had a small furnace for distilling perfumes and herbal essences. These structures seem to have persisted in kitchen gardens into the Victorian age.

By the eighteenth century, vegetable gardens had become fashionable amongst the moneyed classes. The wealth and status of the house-owner was judged by the size of his kitchen garden. The larger the kitchen garden, the more servants and the grander the family it supported. The larger, wealthier households could present peaches, nectarines, melons and pineapples to their dinner guests. Fruit, in particular, was coaxed with great skill to ripen out of season on hotbeds, against walls heated with integral stoves and in hothouses. The formal entrance was in the south wall, but it was just a door: south-facing walls were far too useful to waste on a wide pair of gates. There would have been a side entrance to the east for the cart of dung

from the home farm to be delivered and a cart of produce to be taken up to the house.

The paths from the gates would have dissected the garden into four equal parts. And with the understanding of the importance of crop rotation, each quarter was dedicated in turn to root vegetables, brassicas, and peas and beans and other vegetables. The fourth quarter was sometimes used for potatoes, or left to lie fallow as a space for drying onions and shallots. Permanent crops such as rhubarb, artichokes and soft fruit were grown in strips along the outer edge.

The pavilions were sometimes elaborate enough to house orange and lemon trees, myrtles and oleander in winter. Roses, honeysuckles and jasmine clambered up the walls and around the garden entrances. They were places where the family could sit and enjoy the scents and sounds of flowers and birds. Violets, pinks and marigolds grew to be harvested for herbal remedies and confections. In essence, it was a 'paradise' garden.

The enclosed vegetable garden in winter at Aberglasny, South Wales.

CHAPTER 2

Designs

There can be little doubt that a formally designed vegetable garden is beautiful not just at the height of burgeoning summer, but also in the stark depths of winter. There is an intrinsic satisfaction in the straight lines of symmetrical beds, lines of trained espaliers and neat paths. And the knowledge that each design factor is grounded in considered practicality enhances its appreciation.

In this chapter we take a look at some real ornamental gardens that are in full and fruitful use. Each garden has its own character, its own needs and its own ethos. Every gardener has both different and similar approaches to design, colour and layout. The results are both distinctive and inspirational.

A POTAGER IN RURAL SOMERSET

This private garden is set within a working dairy farm. The farmland has been registered organic with the Soil Association and the natural next step is to register the whole garden too. This will mean that both the beautiful, modern garden of swaying grasses, perennials and shrubs and the ornamental potager within are cultivated on strictly organic lines. The owners, as parents, want to ensure that their young family is raised on produce that has been grown entirely free of pesticides, while as farmers they are aware of the tangible benefits to their cattle

Each formally designed vegetable garden has its own needs and character.

and pasture. Their approach is as scientific as they can make it. Theories are tried out and tested on the ground, quite literally, and if they are proven to be of benefit and to work, they are used. If not, a different organic method is trialled, or a complementary method is added.

The ornamental potager is at a lower level than the buildings to the north, so it is approached down a wide flight of steps. The ground on either side of the steps is supported by a low wall that has been constructed from reconstituted stone blocks.

Tall hornbeam hedges surround the potager, blocking the view from the house and buildings to the north and dividing it from the drive and front garden to the west. The view to the Mendip Hills and fields to the south has been left open. Southerly winds are uncommon and little shade is created.

The design is simple but effective. The beds are rectangular and arranged symmetrically. Looking south, they gradually give way to beds of perennial

The aspect to the south is open.

Decorative ironwork is repeated through the potager.

The layout is formal and symmetrical.

herbs and flowers grown for cutting and simply to decorate the potager. At this juncture, the straight central path opens out into a circle around a central ironwork lotus. Ironwork flowers and artichokes interrupt the skyline, repeating the theme, while decorated arches carry the repetition all along the paths.

The herringbone-patterned brick path of the potager then resolves into formal, mown grass, bordered generously by herbaceous perennials. The design concludes in an experimental bed of tall ornamental grasses (*Stipa gigantea*), interplanted with *Eremurus* 'Cleopatra' that melds the cultivated garden with the fields beyond.

The garden melds into the fields and hills beyond.

A POTAGER WITHIN A LARGER GARDEN

This potager looks decorative year-round.

In a garden that is open regularly to the public, this potager has to look decorative throughout the year. It is visible on two sides from the wider, walled ornamental garden and its rich use of colour draws every visitor to it.

Every bed is edged with boards painted a sumptuous mulberry red that exactly picks up the tones of the outer hedge of *Berberis thunbergii* 'Atropurpurea Nana'. In late summer, this colour is picked up with the dark red dahlia 'Arabian Night' and the tints of ripening apples. Two recycled metal chickens peck beneath the strong green clipped bay, with the twisted ironwork supports toning in rustily. And behind, to the north, the grey stone wall acts as a stage backdrop, setting off the red tones repeated by 'Lollo Rosso' lettuces, beetroot and red cabbages in their season and echoing a dark pewter grey container and silvery cardoons.

The vegetables are chosen not primarily by colour, however, but by the family for the kitchen. They only grow those that they eat. The visual element takes second place, albeit a strong one.

It follows that the family prefers vegetables that have not been sprayed with any chemicals. The garden environment, while not strictly organic, is maintained with care and consideration for birds,

The reds and greys are repeated in the planting.

bees and beneficial insects. Although weedkiller is used on the brick paths for convenience, only soap sprays are used on the vegetables. French marigolds (*Tagetes*) line up beside the peas and beans to control aphids, while coffee grounds are used around vulnerable plants to control the slugs and snails. They appear to work well. Egg shells were tried, but were found to be rather smelly and they disappeared all too quickly into the soil. Snails are a particular problem in this garden with its old, high wall. They like nothing better than snuggling up for the day, or the winter, in the cracks and crevices of the old stonework, biding their time until the warm summer evenings arrive.

Well-rotted horse manure is spread every winter on the vacant beds to feed the soil, and the roots of peas and beans are dug back into the ground after they have finished cropping. The large compost heaps take in leaf litter from the entire garden and their contents are turned and are used on the vegetable garden regularly.

The garden is high on the Mendip Hills and the winds funnel down through the house and outbuildings, joining with the turbulence created by the enclosing wall and often wreaking havoc within the garden. A beech hedge was planted along the west side of the potager to slow down the prevailing wind that funnelled through the

A tall beech hedge on the western side protects the potager from the prevailing winds.

outbuildings behind. This is cut once or twice a year so that in winter the brown foliage is retained in order to provide much needed shelter. In summer, it provides a strong green backcloth for the contrasting reds.

A VILLAGE GARDEN POTAGER

The potager within this smaller village garden remains separate from the rest of the garden while all the time being just visible. Glimpses of its riches are seen through a curtain of perennials under a row of pleached willows. This divides the potager from the lawn and screens the upper windows of the neighbouring houses, giving added privacy to the wider garden. The willows are pollarded each January to keep them under control and the herbaceous planting beneath will retain its skeleton through the winter.

An old stone wall forms the western boundary, topped with stones laid in a traditional 'hen and

A high stone wall forms the boundary.

chickens' formation with stones set vertically in the capping. The high wall totally obscures the neighbouring gardens and provides a silvery-grey backdrop to the planting. All the joints have been regrouted to evict the armies of snails that had taken up residence.

The potager is accessed from the main garden by a path that runs along the southern boundary of the garden. Each bed is 1.2m (48in) wide and the paths are 1m (39in) and 0.8m (32in) wide. The irregular beds are placed symmetrically either side of the centre line and they surround a rectangular bed centred with an old chimney stack.

All the beds and the paths are edged with 2.5cm (1in) thick timber that will not warp and move out of alignment. The paths are finished in gravel with a paver at every corner and at the junctions to mark the changes of direction and the transitions between the potager and the wider garden.

A formal path gives access at the southern corner.

Plan of the potager.

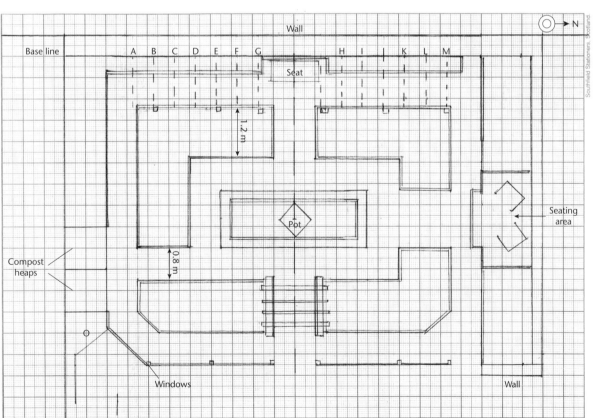

Scale 1:50

A stone paver marks the angle of the access path.

Two compost bins line the north-facing fence. In this position, they are convenient for both the potager and the remainder of the garden. One receives vegetable waste and the other is turned regularly in order to provide organic matter to put on the beds.

The old stone wall that forms the western boundary has been used to grow and fan-train soft fruit in espaliers. Raspberry canes fill the shadier corner space facing north, while sun-loving apricots will be planted and fan-trained to the south-facing wall.

Each small bed has been planted to provide the owner with a succession of fresh vegetables throughout the growing season. The old chimney pot at the centre of the potager provides a focal point from within, and also from outside when looking into the garden.

Annuals are planted in some of the gaps left after harvesting crops so as to encourage insect life and predators, or just to pick for the house. By the late summer they strike a relaxed mood that offsets the garden's intrinsic formality.

A recycled chimney pot forms the centrepiece.

Raspberries fill the shady corner.

Flowers invite insects to the potager.

A battalion of chickens seek out the pests.

A TOWN GARDEN POTAGER

In this charming, quirky town garden, surrounded by hidden neighbours, the owner's sense of humour strikes an informal note. It is a garden that is entirely organic. Both wild and tame life are encouraged to join in the constant battle against slugs and snails, pests and diseases.

Although the vegetable garden is enclosed and out of sight from the main area, it forms another delightful surprise in this garden of unexpected corners. And in this way it is true to the mood of the whole garden.

The potager is separated on one side from the main garden by trellis covered in roses and honeysuckles. A low, 1m (39in) high, fence provides

This scarecrow adds a quirky touch.

A rose-tangled trellis separates the potager from the rest of the garden.

a division from a small pond and an ornamental garden shed. A 2m (79in) wall runs along the east side, and the rear wall of a nineteenth-century stone-built Methodist chapel forms the potager's southern boundary.

The plot is simply laid out around an attractive greenhouse. Its roof finials mimic the ornamental windows of the old Methodist chapel behind. In summer the greenhouse is filled with pots burgeoning with flowers both for the garden and to decorate the potager.

While the chickens are dissuaded from foraging and pillaging the vegetables, they are encouraged to keep down the numbers of pests in the outer garden. The frogs and toads that have hatched in the pond are also enlisted to fight the ongoing

Flowers succeed the seedling vegetables in summer.

The shape of the arch echoes the finials of the greenhouse.

A frog stands sentry duty at the edge of the pond.

A sturdy compost heap brimming with comfrey.

battle against slugs and snails amongst the lettuces and cabbages.

Birds are a mixed blessing. The greedier crows are scared off by the *alter ego* of the owner basking in a deckchair, or a sinister 'hoodie' digging among the hollyhocks.

Against the boundary wall there are two compost heaps that are filled and used on a regular basis, taking care not to disturb any hedgehogs or grass snakes that often take up residence. Although the heaps are distant from the house, they are convenient for the vegetable waste from the potager. Wild comfrey is allowed to seed around and the leaves are added to the heap to provide valuable potassium.

Water butts are placed around the garden wherever there is run-off from a roof, be it from the greenhouse or the shed. This is an Aladdin's cave of old garden tools, out-of-work scarecrows and collections of bottles for making ornamental insets in the paths.

The main paths are simple paving slabs well laid on a bed of sand, and the smaller, narrower paths are gravel. Nasturtiums seed themselves around and by late summer they are invading the space left vacant by earlier crops.

Vegetables have infiltrated other parts of the garden too. Window sills boast hearty cabbages, their silver bloom accented by blue pansies and felty-leaved *Plectanthrus*. In a sunny corner, pots of begonias, pansies and red cabbages are lined out on benches.

A 'hoodie' puts off the birds.

Above and below: lustrous cabbages play a role on the window sills.

The potting shed.

A simple path of paving slabs.

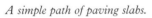

Turkish rocket and herbs to pick for lunch.

The ornamental vegetable beds decorate the transition from functional greenhouses to the wider garden.

And on the conservatory table a pot of Turkish rocket is placed to add to lunchtime sandwiches.

SEMICIRCULAR RAISED VEGETABLE BEDS

In a sloping garden commanding glorious views over the surrounding countryside the ornamental vegetable beds are on display. Above and behind them are greenhouses where early crops of salads are raised in spring and tender vegetables such as fennel, courgettes and tomatoes can be given a warm start. In winter they house special collections of rare plants. Here the ornamental vegetable beds create a decorative transition between the greenhouses and the wider garden.

The original raised bed is rectangular in shape, sited immediately in front of the greenhouses. This 1 × 5m (39 × 197in) plot proved not quite adequate for the family's needs, so the ornamental semicircular bed was added to provide more scope for growing different vegetables. It also made a visual step up to the taller rectangular bed.

Both beds are raised in order to make a level surface, to improve the drainage and to warm up the soil in spring. The semicircular bed is divided into segments like slices of a cake by a herringbone-patterned path of pavers manufactured to resemble 'rustic bricks'. Each path is outlined with specially designed 'rope' edgers.

The beds are raised and terraced.

The herringbone-patterned paths have 'rope' edgers.

The central path is accessed by two simple steps between a pair of stone pillars crowned with large balls, and the other two paths fan out almost to the edge to allow for a newly planted box hedge to develop and grow out.

The central point on the diameter has been raised to accommodate a large pot of mint that would otherwise quickly grow out of control if let loose. The permanent planting has been confined to the two corners. Step-over apples (*see* Chapter 4) are being trained along two of the paths, and to make the maximum use of the space, alpine strawberries line the edges.

The individual beds are planted to provide a succession of vegetables and herbs throughout the year that are never in too great a number to create

A pair of pillars strikes a formal tone.

Step-over apples make good use of the bed space.

a glut. By adding garden compost from the heap nearby, the soil remains in good heart all year.

Details of how to construct this garden are given in Chapter 3.

INFORMAL RAISED VEGETABLE BEDS IN A VILLAGE GARDEN

This modern village garden is on a sloping site overlooking the green valley bottom below. There appeared to be no space for a formal vegetable garden in a potager style, so when the family decided to 'grow their own' the only way was to incorporate it into the existing framework of borders.

The eventual position in the garden was decided by the lean-to greenhouse which could only be sited

The lean-to greenhouse against the garage wall.

against the wall of the garage. The beds were then raised to the horizontal with railway sleepers and pavers were laid to make a sloping path between. Compost heaps were located between the greenhouse and the beds for the sake of convenience.

The garden soil is heavy clay. When the footings were made for the railway sleepers that support the beds, the clay soil was reused to back-fill the resulting terraces. Consequently, the soil is not as free-draining as it should be, so it is constantly being topped up and improved with plenty of compost from the heap. Whenever the beds are being worked on, a plank is laid across the sleepers to prevent footprints from compacting the lower level of clay. And the beds are never dug, as this would bring the clay back up to the surface and would risk capping the soil, so preventing rain from penetrating to the lower levels.

The aim is to grow enough to provide the whole family with vegetables for Sunday lunch throughout the year and with salads up until Christmas. The last sowing of cut-and-come-again lettuces is made in a window box in August. As the nights get colder the lettuce window box is taken into the greenhouse until all have been eaten. To accompany the salads,

A window box of lettuces.

The beds are supported by railway sleepers.

a late sowing of leeks provides thinnings instead of spring onions.

There are always small numbers of a variety of different vegetables growing: mangetouts, purple French beans and just six swedes are grown, for example. In this way, the family never has to cope with a glut and each Sunday roast is accompanied by a different vegetable. Unusual varieties are grown and if they prove unpopular with the discerning family, the small amount means that there are not so many unwanted vegetables to be given away.

The small beds mean that it's possible to spend just the odd hour weeding or planting any given area and so keep the beds tidy. Not only do they provide fresh vegetables, but regular exercise and relaxation too.

Terraced beds, compost heaps and greenhouse.

At the corner of the garden an old Bramley apple tree provides fruit for pies and puddings throughout the winter. The apples are cooked, puréed and frozen, or they are stored for winter in trays in the frost-free garage.

The fence on the shady side of the garden opposite the greenhouse is lined with autumn-fruiting raspberries. These later fruits are remarkably untouched by birds that decimate all red fruits earlier in the summer, so there's no need for unsightly netting.

A stand of sweetcorn makes the transition in late summer to the rest of the garden. It's quite elegant

All sorts of containers are used for sowings of carrots, lettuces and cabbages.

enough to grow for ornament alone, but its fat cobs are testament to their rich upbringing. And a striped garden pot is home to one or two shiny fat cabbages for the winter.

CHOOSING YOUR OWN SITE

Where you position your own potager or less formal ornamental vegetable plot is largely governed by the shape and overall size of the whole garden. But there are one or two essential considerations to take into account before starting.

Size

The first factor is perhaps the most important: that of the overall size of the vegetable-growing element in relation to the garden as a whole. Few domestic gardens are the size of Villandry or Aberglasny, but such grand designs can prove a source of inspiration for smaller gardens. The whole-ground plans will almost certainly be too elaborate for anything smaller than a football pitch. But perhaps a section or corner of the design might be transferrable to a domestic plot. Or maybe the basic ground plan could be simplified by removing some of the internal divisions and making the individual beds proportionately larger.

The ornamental vegetable garden at the Château of Villandry, France.

The guiding principle is that the smaller the garden, the simpler the design. Too many divisions and paths in too small a space mean more dividers and paths than growing area. On the other hand, in a larger garden the beds should be kept small or narrow enough to be able to reach into the middle without having to tread on the soil. And the main paths need to be wide enough for your wheelbarrow.

Light

As do we all, vegetables and most fruit need sunshine. They need plenty of light not only to grow well but also to ripen fruits and flowers. So an open site away from the shade of buildings and trees is preferable.

The north or east side of buildings can be very dark in winter. Often there is a 'rain shadow' effect where the soil is dry beneath a wall even on a wet

Pumpkins can be trained up a slatted fence.

day. It may help to take a few photos of the garden at different times of year just to see which part receives the most light, especially in winter. Usually this area will be facing south or south-east, so that the sunlight falls on it all day. The soil will warm up more quickly in spring and stay warmer as the days get shorter.

So if you have alternative positions, choose the site that avoids the shade of trees, particularly to the south and west. North and east barriers helpfully shelter the garden from colder winds. If the only option is a site that is shadier at one end than the other, then you could choose to grow soft fruit such as raspberries, which are essentially woodland plants, at the shady end and most other vegetables at the brighter, sunnier end.

If the only space you have available is in light shade then grow leafy vegetables rather than peas and beans. They are more successful with less light. And avoid growing too many winter vegetables. They are more vulnerable to fungal disease when the light levels are low between October and March and they may fail to thrive.

Tree roots are also a major problem if the only potential site is under trees. Trying to dig a soil that is matted with roots is very difficult. Cutting through tree roots encourages those roots to grow out again and become very competitive for nutrients and moisture. The tree may be damaged by too much root pruning, or may put on so much growth in response to all those lovely nutrients that it creates even more shade. It's probably better to grow a few ornamental vegetables in pots and containers in the sunniest spot you can find, rather than try to compete with trees.

Wind

Gales and high winds are among the most demoralizing events in any vegetable garden. They knock over stakes, bean poles, sunflowers, sprouts and all. So if the only available site is open to the prevailing wind you should think about protecting it.

In a large garden a windbreak of trees, shrubs or hedging is ideal so long as the roots don't interfere with the vegetables. An access path at the base of the hedge, finished with ornamental bark chippings, allows space for the hedge roots to grow and access to cut the hedge. Or espalier-trained apples and pears could take the place of a hedge, although high winds might knock off the fruit.

Solid fences and walls are a mixed blessing. Often a high wind slams into the outside, is directed up and over the top and causes eddies and mayhem on the inside. The force of the wind could be lessened by attaching low trellising to the top and training strong-growing climbers such as *Clematis montana* to cover it. The growth would soon be thick enough to create a filter, even in winter.

Slatted fencing also helps to prevent this effect by filtering the wind and it could be used to support sweet peas, runner beans or even pumpkins and squashes. Even a low paling fence will provide shelter for smaller-growing vegetables.

Levels

Ideally, any vegetable garden should be on the level. Most vegetables need plenty of moisture at their roots without becoming sodden. If the ground is parched and compacted, the rainwater often runs down sloping ground without really soaking into the soil. Heavy rain can even take away the topsoil in extreme conditions. But providing the soil is not left bare in autumn and winter when you can expect the worst deluges, it should still produce excellent, quality crops.

However, a few factors may need to be taken into account. If the slope faces north it will be cold in winter, but dry, so fungal disease will be less of a problem than in the shade of trees or buildings. The soil will be later to warm up in spring so sowing should be delayed. A cooler aspect means that many peas and beans may take longer to ripen in summer, but vegetables that are inclined to bolt in the heat, such as summer spinach, should produce their leaves for longer. A south-facing slope offers the opportunity to grow more tender vegetables such as globe artichokes and Florence fennel that need a rich, but draining, soil.

On balance, however, growing will be more successful on the level and working will be easier. On a small scale, it's quite simple to install terracing on a sloping site. Railway sleepers or treated timber may not be suitable for the purist organic gardener, but they are practical and available.

Florence fennel grows successfully in a well-drained, raised bed.

On a larger scale, small diggers can be hired at a daily rate, with a driver, for moving soil provided there is access to the site from the road. The terraces can be shored up with horizontal beams of treated timber, then anchored with stout fence posts at regular intervals.

Railway sleepers create simple terraces quickly.

Taller raised beds shored up with timber supports.

A topiary bay tree forms the central focus.

Alternatively, low walls could be installed. They will need to be properly built on foundations and inclined slightly back into the hill. Ideally, the walls should be lined with breeze blocks and small pipes set in the base of the wall at regular intervals, backed with a mesh, to allow for drainage.

Shape

Square and oblong gardens lend themselves well to being divided internally in symmetrical patterns. They are easy to lay out on the ground and quicker and simpler to maintain. Circular features such as a large ornamental pot, a hexagonal arbour, or a topiary bay tree trained into a ball can be set centrally to provide a contrasting focus.

Sometimes a round or semicircular shape fits in better with an informal garden. And then there are different ways of dividing up the inner sections into fan shapes or wedges. Paving stones, bricks and timber blocks may be uncompromisingly square and oblong, with straight sides, but there are slightly curved pavers on the market and bricks are narrow enough to fan out into a circle.

Straight brick-shaped pavers set into a semicircle.

A cottagey mixture of flowers, fruit and vegetables within formal box hedging.

Compost bins within the potager.

Style

Once you have weighed up the opportunities and constraints of the site you have chosen and settled on a pleasing shape, it's time for your imagination to get to work. How do you visualize the finished plot?

Do you want a fully productive garden with neat rows burgeoning with fruit and vegetables? Or do you visualize a happy coexistence for everything in a cottage style, but within formal lines? This lovely jumbled effect needs more attention than it appears. But it does provide a suitable habitat for frogs, hedgehogs, grass snakes: all allies in the war on pests.

What are your feelings about organic gardening? Are you a purist, or would you allow a little compromise here and there to make life easier? Do you want to grow companion crops to encourage hoverflies and natural predators? Would you like to grow flowers for the house? Or would you prefer to produce only vegetables?

Whether you want to garden organically or not, a compost bin or three is essential. It's easier if they are situated near the vegetable garden so that when you pick your cabbages you can just chop off the

outer leaves directly on to the heap. And when you need to use the rotted compost there's no need to barrow it any distance.

Is there enough room for more permanent planting? Would you like to grow perennial vegetables such as artichokes and asparagus? Or soft fruit, or an apple tree? These could all be grown in the main garden if space is at a premium.

Do you want to grow only those vegetables that are in themselves ornamental? Leaf textures and vegetable shapes are marvellous if they are combined with flowers in season. And jumbling them together makes it more difficult for airborne pests to find them, although a nice damp blanket of leaves makes a wonderful concealment for slugs and snails.

What do you think about ornaments in the vegetable garden? A sense of humour certainly does not go amiss among the cabbages and carrots.

And lastly and importantly, how much time do you want to spend on the garden? The answer to this question is never simple. There are peaks and troughs of activity. In the UK the months of March to May are undoubtedly the busiest. The hours spent in spring thoroughly weeding, digging (or not) and manuring (or not) will be long but never wasted. Seed sown will germinate better and young plants will quickly become established and grow away. Thereafter the workload will be lighter, until the winter when it can be as little or great as you wish.

Globe artichokes form a permanent planting.

Ladybirds have a voracious appetite for aphids.

Slugs love a blanket of leaves.

Some snail!

CHAPTER 3

The planning stage

Drawing up plans on paper can seem a little daunting and maybe even unnecessary, but planning the new garden accurately is more easily done with pencil, ruler and, of course, a rubber first. It's very frustrating to discover the snags of your design at a later stage.

Below are two basic plans to illustrate two different designs. The methods can be adapted and used to translate your own ideas on to paper – then the paper plan on to the ground.

PLANNING A FORMAL SQUARE OR RECTANGULAR PLOT

Before you start to work out the plans for your ornamental vegetable garden on paper it's wise to mark out the overall dimensions on the ground. Then you can see how it will look when it's finished.

Choose a sunny winter day when it's possible to see the full extent of any shade cast by the house or trees. You can check if the existing paths give

Working out the layout on the ground (from the north-west).

The layout from the south-east – twine is tied around bricks to make moveable lines.

good, wheelbarrow-friendly access and plants, shrubs and trees that are in the way can be quickly identified. At this stage, you could use pegs or simply lay out canes on the ground, or even railway sleepers, if you have them to use as edgers.

First, decide on your 'baseline'. This is a line from which you take the key measurements. It needs to be outside the overall area of the vegetable garden. You could use the wall of your house, a hedge, a path, or a garden wall. The baseline should extend beyond the total width of the vegetable garden. If this line is obstructed by trees or shrubs then peg down a cord, ensuring that it is straight and at an accurate distance from the wall, hedge or path. Use this as a baseline. (Make sure that it is exactly parallel to the wall, hedge or path that you would have used.)

Take the key measurements from the baseline to the nearest corners of the beds. Use a 30m (100ft) surveying tape to ensure that they are correct. Mark them down on a rough, hand-drawn sketch. Use a metric scale. Even if you usually think in feet and inches, metres are based on the number 10 and are far easier to work with.

Transferring the sketch accurately on to graph paper

- By this time, the sketch will be full of crossings-out and probably a little muddled and muddied.

So take a large sheet of graph paper and decide on the scale. (1cm or 2cm = 1m [1/50] is easiest, but may not always be practical.)

- Work out which direction is north and mark it with an arrow in a corner of the paper.
- Using a scale ruler, draw out your plan accurately on the graph paper.
- Start with the baseline: one end is point 'A' and the opposite end 'P' in this case.
- Divide the baseline into metres, B, C, D, and so on. (The baseline might not be exactly divisible into metres, so note the measurement of the last interval to 'P'.)
- Then mark in the first line of bed corners from the baseline according to those on the sketch of measurements.
- Complete the pattern of beds and paths to scale.

- Take the measurements from the centre (Z) to the point on the baseline opposite the extreme corners of the beds. These lengths should be equal. Note the measurements on the plan (Z–A, Z–O).
- You can use this method of 'triangulation' to locate other features on the plan.
- Complete the plan using a heavier pencil or felt-tipped pen for the baseline and the boundaries, noting down all measurements.

Transferring the plan on to the ground

- Mark the baseline at 1m intervals with pegs (A, B, –P). This will help you to locate the key points and measurements in accurate detail.
- Start by locating the nearest corners (1 and 4) of the overall area by triangulation from the baseline,

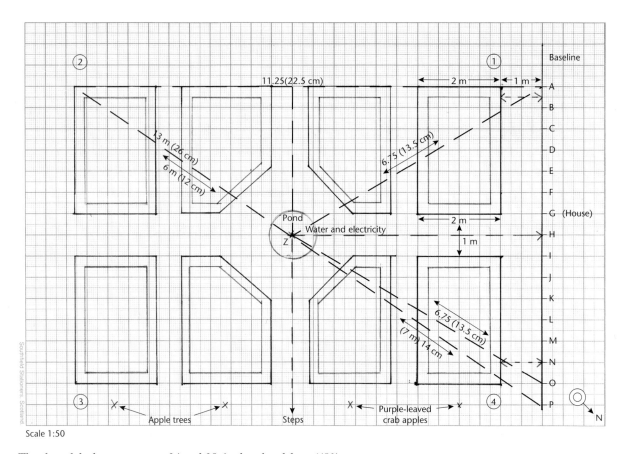

Scale 1:50

The plan of the layout on pages 34 and 35 (scale reduced from 1/50).

using the measuring tape. Mark corners 1 and 4 with a peg that has a nail tapped in on top.

- Then triangulate the furthest corners to ensure that the plot is square, marking them with pegs (2 and 3).
- Tie a line from the corner peg 1 to the nearest peg 2. This forms the sideline of the plot.
- Repeat for the other side (4 and 3). Finish off the rectangle by joining peg 2 to peg 3 with twine.
- Using the same method, find the corners of each of the beds and mark them with pegs and twine.
- Locate the centre point using the triangulation measurements on the plan.
- To make the round central feature, hammer in a strong stake in the middle at point Z with a nail hammered into the top to form a hook.
- Tie a piece of twine to the nail and measure out the exact length of the radius on the twine and tie in another pointed stake at that point.

- Using the stakes like a pair of compasses, draw out a circle on the ground around the centre.
- Mark the circumference more permanently with a can of spray paint or a plastic bag of silver sand with the corner cut off.

Putting in the paths and edges

Now you are ready to put in the footings if necessary for the edges and to prepare the ground for the paths. In the example illustrated, the site was heavily infested with bindweed. This was sprayed off first before covering the whole area with woven plastic membrane to prevent any further bindweed problems. The heavy, treated timber edges will hold their position, but lighter ones could be bolted through the membrane to a concrete plug set in the ground.

Laying out the plan shown on page 36 – the lines are checked by a professional. The blue pipe in the centre is for the water supply to the central pool ('Z' on the plan).

One line has been extended to allow space for the heavy timbers to be laid.

In order to make room for the timbers, the pegs and lines are extended; where the lines cross will mark the corners.

If the paths and edgers are to be laid on to the ground without any membrane, the following method should be used.

- First hammer in pegs at points 1, 2, 3 and 4, checking that they are all level and at the same height as the edgers.
- Dig the footings for the edgers first.
- Insert the footings into a stiff concrete mix: six parts sand to one part concrete. (Only make as much mix as you have time to use; it does not keep.)
- Using pegs 1, 2, 3 and 4, lay the edgers level, square and straight, checking constantly with a builder's level or a spirit level set on the edge of a long board.

All the heavy timbers have been laid and tied in together. Note that the double rows of timbers are overlapped at the corners for extra stability. The beds are being filled with soil from elsewhere in the garden.

- Lay any pavers or slabs on a dry mix of sharp sand and concrete: seven parts sand to one part concrete is ideal.
- Check that there is a slight fall on the path so that the rainwater runs away. A slight crown in the centre of the path will also stop any puddling.
- In the illustrated garden, the membrane paths are to be covered with a 5cm (2in) layer of gravel.

PLANNING A SEMICIRCULAR POTAGER

Raised semicircular beds.

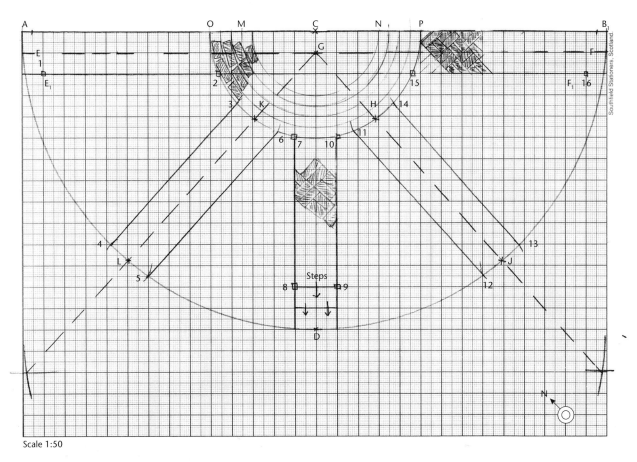

Scale 1:50

The plan of a raised semicircular bed.

Square and rectangular gardens and beds are the simplest to work out on paper and on the ground. Semicircular gardens are more complicated. Bear in mind that the measurements of the paths are especially dependent on the width of the pavers used. It's easier to cut pavers along the width than it is along the length.

Using graph paper, make an accurate plan first (*see* above and illustration). Then, using notched pegs, twine and a 30m (100ft) surveying tape, lay your plan out on the ground. It's worthwhile doing a rehearsal to work everything out on the ground before you start hammering in pegs too firmly.

- Start with a baseline. For a semicircular garden the straight line can be used as a baseline.
- Locate the centre, C, of the baseline, A–B.

- Firmly hammer in a central peg at C and tap in a strong nail to form a hook for radial measurements when making the semicircle.
- Set a line C–D at right angles to the baseline. The line C–D is equal in length to the line A–C.
- From the original baseline at either point A or point B, start a line at 90 degrees by using a 3–4–5 triangle (*see* illustration over the page).
- Next, set a line for the centre of the long path E–F. This path will give access along the back of the beds. Mark E^1–F^1 as the inner edge of this path.
- Find the midpoint G of the line E–F. Using this point G, bisect the two right angles and set lines for the two radial paths (H–J and K–L). Use two stakes and twine as a pair of compasses.

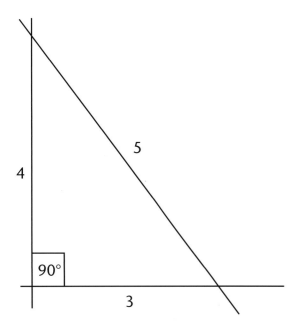

A right-angled triangle. If two sides are in the proportion 3:4, the third side is the distance between the two ends of the lines = 5. The angle between sides 3 and 4 is 90 degrees.

- Next, using point C mark the semicircle M–N. Then similarly mark the semicircle O–P. (Use spray paint to make a more permanent mark.) This will become the inner semicircular path around the focal point at G.
- Mark the semi-circle A–B.
- Set lines at either side of C–D, K–L and H–J to mark the edges of the radiating paths. Make the paths the same width as E–F.

Having pegged out the paths, put in the footings and foundations for the pavers and the edgers. In the example shown, the semicircle is edged with box, so remember to leave the paths about 30cm (12in) short of the edge to allow for planting the box hedge.

Hammer in pegs at points 1–16, checking with a spirit level that they are all at the same height: that of the edgers. The pavers should be laid on a dry mix of sharp sand and concrete as before, while the edgers should be inserted into a stiff concrete mix.

- Start by laying the edgers in the arc M–N. Check they are even with a spirit level laid across the pegs 1–16 on the edge of a board.

HOW TO BISECT A RIGHT ANGLE

- Hammer a stake at point A and tap in a protruding nail.

- Tie a piece of twine to another pointed stake.

- Tie the other end of the twine to the protruding nail, to make a pair of compasses.

- Using the pointed stake, describe an arc that crosses AB and AC.

- Reposition the stake with the nail at point d and make an arc.

- Reposition the stake with the nail again at point e and make another arc

- The arcs cross at point f.

- The line Af bisects the right angle.

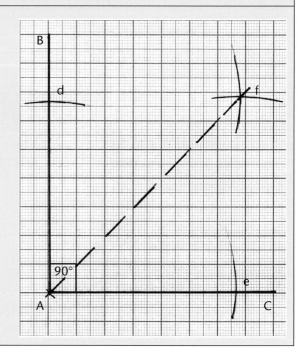

The finished beds in full production later in the summer.

most essential element after the beds: the compost heap. It's too late once the garden is up and running; you will need to make and use compost right from day one.

The most convenient site is as near to the potager as possible. Most of the gardens featured have their composting bins on the perimeter of the actual growing area so that all the vegetable debris can be easily tossed on to the heap and the finished compost is only a short barrow away from where it is needed.

Materials

Compost bins can be made out of recycled treated timber such as old fencing on a demolished wooden shed, providing the wood is still sound. Old pallets can be used for a few years, but you might find their untreated timbers rot down quickly. Or you might want to treat the potager to purpose-built bins made of new treated timber.

Each compost heap should be a minimum 1m (39in) square with stout posts in each corner. Slot boards into the front by placing two more posts 5cm (2in) inside the front two on either side. You could make two or three adjoining heaps at the same time to be filled in succession. It's better to make more separate heaps than one or two very large ones: if they are too big they are slow to heat up and difficult to keep moist.

A permanent composting site could be made out of breeze blocks or reused bricks, but it's a good idea to lay them temporarily for a year. Once they are proven to be in the correct position they can then be cemented in. But whatever you choose for the walls, the floor should not be made of concrete because the compost needs to react with the soil and its organisms.

There are also plenty of prefabricated compost bins on the market that are cheap and easy to use. Most are on a small scale, however, so choose the biggest available. A cubic metre should be the minimum volume for any compost bin if it is to heat up well.

- Then lay a parallel formation of pavers along the arc O–P. Each paver can be slightly turned to describe the curve.
- The remainder can then fill in the path.
- Now the curve O-P provides the baseline for the herringbone paving on all three radial paths. Again, it's worthwhile having a dry run to discover the snags.

Finally, once the paths have been laid for about a week, it's time to brush in some dry sand to infill the cracks. Then you can begin to prepare the beds for planting.

COMPOST HEAPS

While the ornamental vegetable garden is still at the planning stage it's easier to find room for the

Turning the heap

If you can spend a warming hour forking the contents of the first bin into the second bin it will speed up the composting process. And if you add a layer of 'accelerator' every 30–45cm (12–18in) that will hasten the decaying process even more.

But it's not essential to turn the heap frequently. If you cap a full bin with a layer of farmyard manure or straw and an old piece of carpet, the worms and all the other busy organisms will do a lot of the work for you, although it will take them longer.

GREENHOUSES

Even if you are only considering having a greenhouse, it is as well to work out a suitable location before you start. It would be frustrating to find after you have laboured to construct a beautiful potager that it would have been better had it been a few metres to the right to make room for a greenhouse.

Although a greenhouse is not absolutely necessary, it is supremely useful for starting off seedlings and stealing a march on the seasons. And by the summer, once all the burgeoning vegetable plants have been placed in the garden, it becomes the ideal place for growing tomatoes, peppers, aubergines and so on.

The argument for spending money and erecting an attractive greenhouse that is visible from within the potager is strong, but it is an expensive piece of equipment. It may be possible to place a cheaper, more utilitarian greenhouse somewhere else in the garden. Or another alternative might be to embellish a plain wooden greenhouse with curlicues and finials; or paint it a different colour. Then, of course, there are probably cool window sills, porches or conservatories where seedlings and outdoor tomatoes could be raised in the spring. But they do have their limitations of space, temperature and cleanliness, and not all members of the family might want to share their rooms with trays of seedlings, soil and the inevitable greenfly.

However, should you bite the bullet and install a greenhouse you will be unable to understand how you thought you could have managed without it. And if it is as decorative as the potager around it, it will certainly make a very positive contribution to the garden.

The golden rule when buying a greenhouse is to choose one that is as big as you can accommodate

A traditional-shaped greenhouse for raising young plants in spring and growing tender vegetables in summer.

and afford, although it should not take up a disproportionate amount of space in relation to the vegetable beds around or alongside it. If you plan to keep it frost-free, it would be wise to bear in mind the costs of heating; they always rise (though there are ways around this problem – *see* below).

Domestic greenhouses do not usually need planning permission, but check with the local Planning Department first, especially if it will be large in proportion to the ground area of the house.

Siting

If the greenhouse is to be located within or near the potager, it will almost certainly be in a suitably sunny location. Just like vegetables, the greenhouse needs to be somewhere light and protected from the prevailing wind. Trees can be a hazard to glass: whereas a falling branch will damage a row of cabbages, it could demolish a greenhouse. Trees also rob the light. Seedlings, tomatoes, aubergines and so on will tend to grow long, thin and unhealthy if the greenhouse is in shade. Frost pockets are another hazard, especially in the colder areas of the country. Frost tends to run downhill, to be trapped by a wall or fence, and if the greenhouse is in the way, the heating costs will rocket.

Heating and power

Another consideration is whether and how the greenhouse is to be heated. The nearer it is to the house the easier it will be to install power for heating and, perhaps, lighting. If it's very close, a power cable could be run overhead. Otherwise it will be a matter of running a subterranean cable before starting work on the potager. It's also useful to remember

that the further away the greenhouse is from the domestic power supply, the more power is lost. As with all electrical work, it's essential to get professional advice and to have power installed by a registered electrician.

Shape

An ornamental greenhouse does not have to be rectangular with a pitched roof. It could be a 'lean-to' greenhouse against the house or garden wall. It might be positioned to enjoy the radiated heat of the house wall in winter and minimize the cost of heating. However, if a lean-to greenhouse covers a house or garage doorway, then the glazing must conform to British Standard regulations over toughened glass.

A lean-to greenhouse against a wall.

Materials

Treated timber and cedar wood are the most appropriate and decorative materials for the frame of a greenhouse. It's difficult to make extruded aluminium look ornamental. Treated timber could be painted and ornamented, but it would require regular painting. However, that might be an opportunity to try different colours of paint, or to change the finials. Cedar, on the other hand, is durable and slow to rot; nor would it need to be treated or painted. The colour would remain a soft orange-brown, with a lovely natural scent.

Glass

If the greenhouse glass is to extend to the ground it would be wise to consider the extra expense of using toughened glass. This is especially important when the family includes small children, footballs and exuberant dogs; and cleaning the panes from a pair of stepladders is only safe if toughened glass is used. Toughened glass shatters like a car windscreen, into thousands of granules. It should meet the BS6206 Class A standard.

Water butts

Placing a water butt beneath the downpipe is another useful extra to consider. Rainwater can be used to irrigate maturing vegetables. Seeds and seedlings, however, are safer with mains water, as there is the danger that waterborne fungal diseases from the roof could sit in the water butt and make more of themselves. The lid should be kept on the butt at all times too, in order to prevent leaves and debris from souring the water.

Ventilation

If you are buying a new greenhouse it would be worth paying for extra ventilation in the form of additional opening windows. Louvres would be useful too, although mice and, in country areas, small rabbits can easily hop through an open louvre and demolish the contents of the greenhouse in a night. Young plants and seedlings need plenty of air circulating around their stems to keep away damping off, while on hot summer days the greenhouse could become so tropical that even the tomatoes might wilt. Automatic vent and window openers are also available; these are very useful if you expect to be out all day in the summer. They are relatively cheap gadgets that save a lot of worry.

Floor

The floor of the greenhouse could consist of bare earth, or concrete. Traditional gardeners would plant tomatoes directly into the soil alongside a central path – that is, until the tomatoes succumb one year to a build-up of soil-borne diseases. An alternative is to cover the earth with a woven membrane that suppresses the weeds, topped off with a 5cm (2in) layer of horticultural grit. Weeds love to seed

A water butt fed from the roof of a garden shed.

themselves into grit, however. On balance, a concrete floor is easier to sweep, keep clean and damp down on hot days.

Staging

Greenhouse staging is usually available from the manufacturer and delivered at the same time as the frame and glass. It therefore fits precisely and matches the materials of the greenhouse. Alternatively, you could buy cheaper aluminium staging, which, from the outside, cannot be seen under the wealth of plants. Cover the staging with capillary matting to act as a reservoir of moisture for your seedlings in between watering. If you immerse the end of the matting into a container of water the moisture will be drawn up like a wick and may be sufficient to keep young plants going for a day or two if you are away.

Heating

Heating a greenhouse can be very expensive. It pays to insulate the glass with bubble plastic, which can be fitted easily and quite cheaply in autumn. It will save far more than its cost if you are planning to keep the temperature above freezing in winter. But don't be too economical. Reusing the bubble plastic year on year tends to increase the number of bugs and beasties taking advantage of its warmth.

There may be no need for the entire greenhouse to be kept frost-free. An internal partition can be installed to divide the space and keep just one end heated. It might appear very expensive to keep even this space heated on a sub-zero night, but in the context of all 365 days, there are probably only a few nights of the year that are cold enough for the heating to come on. The glass itself should keep off between 3–4°C of frost.

Electric fan heaters controlled by a good thermostat distribute warm air throughout the space very effectively and are simple and safe to use. Set the thermostat to at least 4°C to allow for the warm air to cool as it reaches the corners furthest away from the heater. Circulating the air also helps prevent the fungal diseases that are so common in tightly closed greenhouses.

There are paraffin and propane gas heaters available too, but they can be awkward to use and have the tendency to run out in the middle of a freezing night. Electric radiant heaters are cheap and easily available for a small greenhouse or a partitioned-off section, but they do not circulate the air effectively.

COLD FRAMES

Greenhouses constructed on a low wall offer the opportunity to build cold frames along the side; cold frames are extremely useful to all vegetable growers. They offer a protected space that is a halfway house between the greenhouse and the open beds. And if there is no greenhouse, they create enough protection to start vegetables off a little early, or make the transition from the warmer temperatures of an indoor window sill or porch.

The low wall of a greenhouse makes an ideal site for a cold frame.

Shapes

Some cold frames are at least as attractive as an ornamental greenhouse. The traditional shape against a wall is rectangular and taller at the back than the front: that is, pent-shaped. The lids can be propped up, or removed completely as required. They can also be closed up tight and secured with a catch, which is important on windy days and frosty nights. Use toughened glass on cold frames: they are at the same level as boisterous children and bouncy dogs.

Tall frames can be sited against any sunny south- or west-facing wall. They are shallower from front to back than the conventional low frames, thereby offering shelving at different levels. Just like a lean-to greenhouse, a house wall could provide radiated warmth and a level of frost protection.

Construction

Inside, the floor surface could be either concrete or membrane and grit. Either way, it's important to keep it level and even. Screw the frame down firmly to battens if that is possible. Not only will the wind be unable to shake it, get underneath and blow it away, neither will marauding mice: these have surprisingly flat heads that can squeeze through the narrowest of cracks.

POTTING SHEDS

If you have the space, a potting shed built near the ornamental vegetable garden is a wondrous thing. You can store just about all the equipment and tools

The potting shed.

you need in one. It's ideal for sowing, pricking out and potting up vegetable seedlings. And with an electric light and a radio it quickly becomes a snug retreat from the spring rains where you can potter for hours.

But some garden sheds are not very pretty and often it's the inherited ones that are the least attractive. Like a run-down old house, however, a thorough cleaning and a lick of paint can work wonders. And sheds, like greenhouses, contract in size with use: the more you use them, the less space there seems to be. So choose one that is at least as big as you think you will need.

Constructing a new shed

Construction of a new shed can be carried out by the manufacturer provided that a base is in place before delivery. If the shed is to have a timber floor rather than a concrete one, the base will need to be level and square and well compacted with hardcore. Concrete is easier to keep clean, but a wooden floor is more comfortable on the feet. Unless you have lined walls, the shed is unlikely to be reliably frost proof, so onions and dahlia tubers will probably need to be stored elsewhere.

Equipment

Once a new shed is in place, or an old one has been restored, you can fit a potting bench along one side using a sheet of tannalized timber fixed to the wooden walls. Include upright posts for stability: the bench is going to hold lots of damp, heavy compost and trays of seedlings. Shelving is useful for storing pots and seed trays, plant foods and sprays. Keep garden chemicals on the highest shelf out of the reach of small children.

USEFUL AND ESSENTIAL GARDEN TOOLS

Once you have the garden shed sorted out, it will provide somewhere to store the lawnmower, wheelbarrows and all the tools you will most definitely need. Some garden tools are the sandwich makers of the gardening world: just gizmos. If you start off with the basics, all gadgets can be added to your collection as and when they are needed.

Spades, forks and shovels

It's a false economy to buy cheap spades and forks. If the shafts are made of light, inferior materials, they will have a short life and you will have to replace them quite often, especially if you do not live in an area of sandy soil.

A good quality border spade and fork that are well balanced, with strong shafts and handles, should last a lifetime. Smaller 'ladies' spades and forks are useful, but not essential, for lighter jobs or working in tight corners. There are also the American-style spades and forks available these days with long shafts and no handles. They use the principle of leverage to turn the soil over: a different technique that may suit your style of digging, especially if your back is troublesome. Keep them clean and hang them up in the shed after you have used them. If they are left out in the rain, frost and snow, they will deteriorate.

Shovels are cheap and useful for moving piles of manure. There are long-handled versions of these too if you prefer.

Rakes and hoes

A strong rake is a must for preparing seedbeds, while a good quality hoe is essential for beheading weeds between the rows. Long-handled draw hoes cut on the pull, while on lighter soils Dutch hoes can be pushed more easily. Oscillating hoes cut on both strokes. Those that are attached to the shaft with a riveted tang are the least likely to lose their own heads, although they are more expensive.

Hand tools

Trowels and hand forks are less expensive than spades and border forks. Two-pronged hand forks seem to be more useful for getting out intractable weeds from between rows of onions; those with three prongs seem to disturb the ground too widely. Of all hand tools, these are the most easily left on the compost heap, or tossed on the bonfire in a bucket of weeds. They may not be disposable, but they are too often disposed of. So, if you need to economize, you could buy the cheaper versions. If they have brightly coloured handles they are less likely to be lost; otherwise, you could stick on some red or yellow tape.

A dibber is another useful tool. It is simply made out of an old spade handle or something similar. It should be about 30cm (12in) long, with a handle at one end and the other end sharpened to a blunt point. It's especially useful for making holes for young transplanted leeks.

Stakes, lines and labels

A stake and line is very useful for marking out straight rows, but not entirely essential. It's easy to use two canes and a ball of string as an alternative.

And having sown a straight line, it helps to have some plant labels to hand so as to identify what you have planted. Indelible pens are rarely totally weatherproof, but a soft pencil works perfectly well and for long enough.

Hire tools

There exists a special tool or machine for almost every job in the garden. Whether or not to buy any of them depends upon how much you will use them. For example, it's cheaper to hire a really big rotavator that will drive itself along easily without lots of tiring pushing, rather than buy and accommodate a lighter one that will still require no small amount of effort to use. There's only so much room in a garden shed.

CHAPTER 4

The basic materials

DIVISIONS AND EDGERS

While it is not essential to divide a potager from the rest of the garden, it may look better if this is the case. In addition, a wall, fence or hedge does make it more difficult for larger garden pests to get in. Your choice of material often dictates the overall style and mood of the interior; ideally, it should also relate to the garden as a whole.

The paths are the arteries of the garden. Any sudden change of hedging or fencing, or difference in style, makes a break in the flow as you move through the garden. The repetition within the potager of elements in the wider garden relates the one to the other, unifying the overall garden design. Even if the vegetable garden is separate and screened off completely from outside, it still needs to feel connected. It should still be a part of the whole.

Those Victorian walled vegetable gardens were hidden away, out of view from the house. The walls were proof against marauders, as well as creating microclimates within for all sorts of fruit and produce. However, if walls do not already exist, they would be extremely expensive to build.

Fences and hedges are much more affordable and they too have practical advantages. They create shelter from the wind in an exposed garden. Fruit can be trained along and up a fence, while in country gardens rabbit-proof meshing can be buried outside an openwork fence as it is being erected. It should be a fine 1cm or ½in mesh: young rabbits have very small skulls and great appetites.

Rabbit-proof fencing can also be incorporated into the middle of a hedge when it is planted, or you could use viciously barbed *Berberis* to deter the thumpers. It will need to be cut once or twice a year according to the species used.

Box and yew are evergreen and slow-growing, requiring only an annual cut. Yew is poisonous to most mammals, including cattle and horses but excluding deer. Box is also toxic to all mammals, even to deer, but it can make high-density housing for overwintering snails.

Beech and hornbeam are not evergreen, although if they are cut annually the dead leaves remain on the hedge throughout the winter. Beech can be 'greedy': competing for nutrients and water, while not tolerating heavy soils. Hornbeam is less

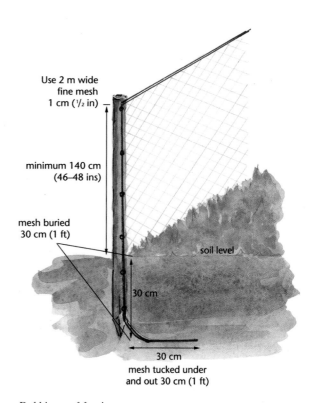

Use 2 m wide
fine mesh
1 cm (½ in)

minimum 140 cm
(46–48 ins)

mesh buried
30 cm (1 ft)

soil level

30 cm

30 cm
mesh tucked under
and out 30 cm (1 ft)

Rabbit-proof fencing.

competitive and will grow happily on most soils that are not extremely dry or waterlogged.

Privet is greedy and usually drops most of its leaves after Christmas. It also needs cutting at least twice a year, if not more. *Lonicera nitida* is evergreen and not especially competitive, although it grows very quickly and would need cutting two or three times a year.

But a truly ornamental vegetable garden does not need to be cut off visually from the house. It could be incorporated openly into the garden, especially in urban gardens where rabbits are not a problem.

The styles of divisions within the vegetable garden, however, can be many and various. Each

The vegetables and fruit could meld seamlessly into the wider area in urban gardens.

Hornbeam hedging.

may need to be considered for practicality, cost and ease of maintenance.

Box (*Buxus sempervirens*)

Lines of clipped box hedging have a classical image that immediately lends structure to an ornamental vegetable garden. They speak of elegant parterres, French potagers and formal Victorian beds.

Box is evergreen and grows so slowly that it only needs clipping once a year, in May or June after all danger of frost has passed. If it is clipped too early the new growth can get blackened by late frosts in April and May. But clipping a low box hedge is hard on the back with or without a mechanical hedge trimmer. It's a factor that should be taken into account.

Over the past few years box blight has become a major problem. If you already have some box in the garden that is free of the disease it would be well worth going to the trouble of taking your own cuttings a year or two ahead of time. Side shoots will root easily if they are taken with a heel in October, potted up in spring and grown on in pots.

However, in country gardens pheasants can be quite a nuisance, especially in spring. The males seem to like snapping off and pulling out young box and tossing the shoots in the air. Perhaps they are trying to impress their ladies. They don't impress gardeners. Although box does seem to be poisonous to most animals including rabbits and deer, the leaves do make snug shelters for snails. They are just biding their time, waiting to sample the vegetable delights you are growing for them.

Box hedges can also harbour pernicious weeds. Make sure that the ground is thoroughly clear of perennial weeds before the hedge is planted and pull out any that have seeded into the base regularly.

Dwarf Lavender or Santolina

Silver-leaved shrubs are more suitable than box for a well-drained soil in sun. They are also ever-grey

Low box hedging.

Lavandula 'Hidcote'.

the flower stalks fade. *Santolina chamaecyparissus* has aromatic, silver foliage and rather brassy yellow buttons. However, if the flowers displease they can be avoided by trimming the hedge in April and thereby removing the flower buds. This will also keep the hedge much tidier. *Santolina neapolitana* 'Edward Bowles' has cream buttons that are easier on the eye, although by leaving them to flower the hedge does then become rather untidy. Trim this hedge in midsummer after the flowers have faded.

Both santolina and lavender are faster growing than box, but whereas box will last for generations, silver-leaved shrubs have a short lifespan. They will probably need renewing every six to ten years. By this time, too, they will have become woody at the base and gappy enough to allow weeds to get a hold within the hedge. Digging the hedge up and starting again is the best remedy.

Espalier or cordon apples and pears

In many of the traditional vegetable gardens apples and pears were trained on to a wall in parallel lines: espaliers. This causes the horizontal branches to 'break' and thus produce more fruiting points.

Cordon apples grown at a 45° angle.

and produce flowers. Dwarf lavenders make particularly attractive hedges. There are three of note: the deep purple-flowered *Lavandula* 'Hidcote'; *L.* 'Hidcote Pink'; and mauve *L.* 'Munstead Dwarf'. They all grow to about 45–60cm (18–24in) and are very attractive to bees. However, rabbits, deer and slugs and snails do not appear to find them palatable.

Santolina, or Cotton Lavender, produces button flowers in summer, but can get a little straggly as

But there is no need to pin an espalier to a wall. It will often grow better if it is free standing, and makes an attractive boundary to a vegetable garden.

Single-stemmed, cordon apple trees can also be trained to grow at an angle. A row of parallel, angled cordons would also make an effective visual boundary. Both are permanent, long-lived structures that produce plenty of fruit provided they are pruned correctly in late summer. However, if they are left unpruned they grow out and become rather strangely shaped trees.

A line of herbs or low-growing flowers such as chives or Poached Egg Plants could be grown beneath without competing for nutrients and moisture with the fruit. The weeding is simple, but it is an ongoing job.

Step-over apples and pears

Over the past twenty years fruit-tree growers have developed the technique of bending down columnar apple or pear varieties horizontally to the ground: step-overs. They can be trained at knee or thigh height and are especially suitable for a smaller garden. They too produce lots of fruit in a small

Step-over apples.

Chives.

space, but they also need to be pruned correctly in late summer, or they will also grow out and become little monsters.

Chives (*Allium schoenoprasum*)

Although chives are not evergreen, they have a presence for much of the year. They produce pink, white or, more usually, mauve flowers in summer, and these are even more delicious to eat than the chopped leaves.

Chives tend to suppress the weeds, though they themselves are quite invasive self-seeders. They also have the disadvantage of harbouring diseases, especially rust, that could transmit to onions and leeks growing in the garden.

Brick

The perfect match for a herringbone brick path is a brick edging. It is laid with the corner upmost. The mellow colours are sympathetic with all growing plants. Brick corners could be laid outside

Brick edgers.

Woven edgers with variegated thyme.

hedges or rows of chives, or they look perfect on their own.

Real house bricks may harbour slugs and snails in their indentations (their 'frogs'), but purpose-made brick pavers have a smooth finish. House bricks, too, are not frost hardy unless they are laid correctly with only the edges exposed, as if they were in a wall. Otherwise the frost and rain will fracture them. This may well be perceived as a positive feature, like the patina on an antique table, but it is a factor to consider.

Woven willow

Although they have a rustic, cottagey look, woven willow edgers are very short-lived. You should expect to replace them after three or four years at the most.

But they are cheap and easy to put in and are sufficient, if temporary.

They do not compete for moisture and nutrients with the growing vegetables, but they might harbour snails over the winter in their nooks and crannies. And make sure the willow does not grow: it roots out very easily if the wood is freshly cut. Not only would willow make a fast-growing hedge that would have to be cut back every few weeks, but it would soak up the moisture with a great thirst.

Treated timber edgers

There is something very pleasing about a timber edge to straight-sided beds. It neatly accentuates the lines, especially in winter. And if it is pressure-treated it will last in contact with the soil for up to ten years.

Unlike living hedges, timber does not compete for moisture and nutrients with the vegetables, so they can be grown right up to the edge of the beds. It also allows for a deep layer of organic matter to be worked into the beds, or a surface mulch, without spilling over. But if, after a time, it begins to warp, slugs and snails can squeeze down the gaps and lay their eggs to await a spring foraging expedition. The thicker the timber the less it will warp; however, the thicker the timber, the more expensive it is.

Thoroughly organic gardeners may find treated timber unacceptable, but if the timber has not been treated it will rot down within a few years and will need to be replaced.

RAISED BEDS

As we have seen, the beds can be raised using old railway sleepers laid horizontally, or heavy, treated timbers can be bedded in vertically. Alternatively, but at greater expense, stone or brick walls, lined with breeze blocks, are more permanent. These are both big operations on a large scale requiring professional help and possibly access for heavy machinery from the road.

On a sloping site, raising one side to form a terrace will level out the beds, making them much easier to work on. Raising a bed by just 30cm (12in) is enough to allow for much better drainage if the garden soil is heavy and unworkable. And because the soil level is raised and draining, it warms up faster in the spring, thus allowing for earlier crops.

If raised beds are constructed, they will have to be filled with topsoil and that can be quite a variable element. Ask advice from gardening neighbours before choosing a topsoil merchant from the phone book. Topsoil is scraped in layers off old fields or sites designated for building. The topmost layer is usually more expensive than what can often amount to just subsoil, which is virtually sterile. Your vegetables will not grow as well, however much you try to improve subsoil.

Wooden edgers.

Raised beds made of heavy treated timber.

PATHS

The choice of materials for making the paths between the beds can make or mar even the most ornamental gardens. Muddy tracks between the beds look messy and attract weeds. And a barrow wheeled along too narrow a path knocks into the vegetables and breaks up the edges. So it's sensible to make the main paths wide enough for a wheelbarrow and the inner paths not so narrow that you cannot put down a bucket of weeds. The beds themselves are easier to work on if you can reach the middle from the path without stepping on the soil.

If the surface of the path is brick or compressed aggregate and has a slight 'crown' so that the water drains off at either side it will not puddle or become waterlogged. Alternatively, if you decide on flagstones, you could angle them slightly for drainage.

Bricks or pavers

Probably the classic path in an ornamental vegetable garden is one made of recycled bricks laid in a herringbone pattern. It is a warm terracotta colour that works well with most coloured foliage and flowers. It hints at the reuse of materials used in an earlier building; of nostalgia for cottage gardens and a gentler time. Nowadays, though, machine-made pavers that weather the frost and rain are readily available and within a few years will lose their rawness. However, brick or paver paths can become uneven and slippery as moss builds up on their surface, while the joints can attract weeds and hide slugs and snails. In addition, this type of path can be expensive.

The bricks or pavers are bedded in a herringbone pattern into builders' sand and a dry-mix concrete. If you are doing this yourself it's worth laying them out first as a trial, as it's easy to miscalculate the quantities. Ensure that the finished path has a slight crown so that the rain will drain off; frost will downgrade recycled brick even faster if it remains wet. Or you could use a mixture of bricks or pavers and some other material such as gravel or stone slabs. This combination is particularly effective on right-angled corners.

Recycled brick path.

Pavers.

Patterned pavers.

Pavers laid in a semicircle.

In the semicircular garden, the pavers are each laid at a very slight angle to describe the curve of the semicircle. It's worth checking the quantities by laying them out first as a dry run. It's not good to run out when the dry-mix bed is already down, or it may set before you can start again.

Shaped pavers are available to make circles of different sizes. Lay them with the long side along the circumference. Usually the manufacturers will provide a chart to help calculate the quantities and shape you need.

Paving slabs (45cm/18in square).

Paving slabs

Reconstituted stone or concrete paving is quick and easy to lay on a bed of builders' sand and dry-mix concrete. On the whole they work out cheaper than recycled bricks or pavers, but the quality and price varies widely. The more you pay for them, the longer their lifespan. Choose those with a textured surface to prevent them becoming slippery on wet days.

Modern slabs are usually 45cm (18in) square. Larger sizes tend to be unmanageable and hard on the back. But the dimensions do dictate the width of the path. Lay them out first to see whether and how many slabs will need to be cut, for which it's worth hiring a special machine. It will save time and broken slabs. When you lay them properly, tilt them slightly off the horizontal. That way the rain drains off the surface more efficiently.

Gravel

Coarse gravel paths are more adaptable in shape than bricks, pavers or slabs. The gravel can be laid directly on to a smooth surface of soil, or a dry-mix concrete. There is also the option of laying gravel on to black plastic membrane. This allows moisture to penetrate while preventing weeds from growing through, although it does tend to shred at the edges into long, narrow ribbons of black plastic that are dangerous to small animals and birds. So tuck the edges of the membrane beneath the edging of the path; edging is necessary anyway to prevent the gravel from kicking up on to the beds or into the surrounding garden. Note that this type of material does not break down into the soil for centuries.

Weeds and self-seeding garden flowers particularly like to grow in gravel. At present, there are weedkillers on the market that can be applied once or twice a year to prevent this problem, but there is no organic alternative and legislation may change regarding the use of weedkillers.

CHAPTER 5

Getting down to earth

Once the framework of the ornamental vegetable garden, the paths and edges, has been laid, it's time to prepare the ground. Ideally, it's best to start work in the autumn. In the months ahead the soil will benefit from a period of frost and rain to break it up and settle it down before the business of sowing and planting begins in the spring.

ANALYSING THE SOIL

When someone asks what sort of soil your garden has, it can be puzzling. It's brown. It grows weeds. It's wet when it rains. What more is there to soil? An expert gardener's answer might run to pages, but there are a few basic questions to ask yourself.

Getting the beds ready in autumn.

Firstly, is the soil sticky? When it's dry does the surface develop deep cracks? When you squeeze a handful then release it, does it hold its shape? Could you mould it into pots? And when you rub it between your fingers and thumb, does it feel smooth and silky? If so, the soil is probably silt or clay. It has very fine particles that hold the moisture, but once it has dried out it becomes solid. Clay soil is very hard work initially, but in time, once it has been prepared and conditioned for a few years, it will prove the most fertile soil of all.

Or, does a handful of soil run through your fingers? When it rains does the surface become dry again within hours? Is it impossible to make it into balls? When you rub it in your fingers, does it feel gritty? If so, it's a sandy soil. It has coarse particles that drain the moisture away quickly. Even after a deluge, the soil will be dry enough to work on within a day or two. But nutrients also drain away fast with the water and plants desiccate quickly in dry weather. It will always need plentiful additions of organic matter to act like a sponge and hold the moisture in the soil for the plants.

Or is your soil neither of the above? Does it make a ball in your fist, but crack up easily and break apart quickly? If it feels neither smooth and silky, nor gritty, it is loam. This is perhaps the easiest soil to work and repays all your labours if it is maintained with plenty of organic matter.

Topsoil and subsoil

Soils, however, change their composition at different depths. In the gardens of old houses where the soil has been worked for centuries by generations of conscientious vegetable gardeners, there will be a great depth of topsoil. But in newer gardens the topsoil can be quite shallow.

And what happens in the subsoil will directly affect the ground surface. For example, sometimes the topmost level is a rich, fertile loam, but lower down it becomes solid, sticky clay. In heavy rain, the surplus water drains away very slowly because of the impermeable clay subsoil and the garden quickly becomes boggy. It's when you understand the structure of the soil at different levels that you will be able to understand how it works in your own patch.

The simplest way to discover the structure of your soil is to insert a spade straight down. Remove the soil so that you are left with a cubic hole with vertical sides. Take a close look at the vertical face of the soil. The topsoil layer will be dark brown or black. It will have roots, bugs and beasties in it. Beneath the topsoil layer the colour will change probably quite suddenly. It may be paler. There will be no roots or wildlife living in it. It's the infertile

A stony loam soil.

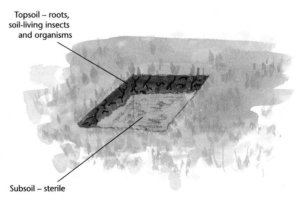

Topsoil – roots, soil-living insects and organisms

Subsoil – sterile

Soil profile.

subsoil. The topsoil can be clay, sand or loam, but the subsoil could be quite different. Once you know what the topsoil and subsoil are each composed of, you can draw conclusions about the depth of the fertile topsoil and the drainage.

Buried horrors

In the gardens of new-build houses and sometimes in old houses too, there can be all sorts of horrors buried beneath the surface: bricks, roof felting, even old washing machines.

Barn conversions often have the old farmyard as a garden. The builders may have broken up the yard concrete, then buried the lumps. All this will have to be laboriously removed before you can begin. Or the yard may have been buried with its concrete surface intact. Or there may be no concrete, but the ground has been trampled for centuries by animals and the subsoil has become compacted. This is called a 'pan'. A buried panned layer, whether it's concrete or compacted earth, will bring all sorts of frustrating problems when you try to grow anything over it. It will act like an enormous tea tray, so that the rainwater will be unable to run away and will collect like spilt tea. Or in a sunny summer the soil will dry out like a crisp biscuit on a griddle. This is a problem that needs tackling at the outset with a deep ploughshare in order to break up the pan, if at all practical.

The pH of your soil

The pH scale is a measure of the alkalinity or acidity of the soil. For 'alkaline' read 'lime'. There's probably no real need to test your soil to discover its exact pH. Take a look around at other people's gardens in the area. If your neighbours can grow healthy, green-leaved rhododendrons, camellias and blue-flowered hydrangeas, then your soil is likely to be quite acid. If the hydrangeas are pink and red and there is no sign of rhododendrons, azaleas or camellias, then the soil is probably alkaline. Vegetables, on the whole, prefer a more alkaline soil.

So on acid soils it's beneficial to sprinkle lime on the soil according to the directions on the packet. If you have acid clay it will have the effect of breaking it up, but it's important not to do this at the same

THE pH SCALE

pH is shorthand for indicating the levels of acidity and alkalinity in the soil. These levels are given in a scale from 0–14, where 7 is theoretically neutral (in fact, a pH of 6.5 is effectively neutral for plants). The lower the number, the more acidic the soil; the higher the number, the more alkaline.

It is a logarithmic scale; that is, each change of number is an increase or decrease by a factor of 10. So, for example, pH5 is 10 times more acidic than pH 6. And pH5 is 100 times more acidic than pH7.

time as spreading the organic matter (*see* below). Let a few months pass first. All soils will gradually become more acid as you spread organic matter, especially manure. So it's wise to give a light dressing of lime every few years even on alkaline soils.

PREPARING THE GROUND

Once any basic problems have been sorted out and the ground levelled, the soil structure and texture analysed, the next step is to prepare the soil for planting. At this point there are two options: to use organic methods, or to compromise.

Getting rid of the weeds

The organic method of cleaning the ground of weeds is to cover it entirely with woven plastic matting or old carpets for at least one year. This will starve the weeds of light and they should, in theory, expire (*see* Chapter 10).

It may be tempting to take a short cut and start forking out the perennial weeds. However, they have lots of tricks up their shoots. Many, such as bindweed, dandelions, docks, couch grass and ground elder, regrow from the tiniest piece of root left in the soil. By merrily forking and digging the area you are doing them a favour: propagating them by their roots. You will end up thinner and fitter, but with an area even more affected with pernicious weeds than before.

The pragmatic, non-organic alternative is to spray the whole area with a translocated weedkiller. This affects everything that is green: leaves, stems and all, then moves down the weed to kill it off at the roots. If you spray in the autumn some weeds will return in spring; the area can be sprayed once again until it is quite clear. Translocated weedkillers work only on green matter. Once they come into contact with soil particles the active chemicals bind to the particles by ionization while they gradually break down harmlessly.

To dig or not to dig?

Many gardeners advocate a 'no-dig' method whereby organic matter is simply laid on the surface of the soil and the worms are left to pull it down over the winter. This is certainly a good method to use in established beds, but it may prove unsuitable for a new garden. Here, the soil could have become compacted, or squashed down, from repeated walking, or even mowing if it was a lawn. Soil should have air pockets for healthy root growth. And those recalcitrant weeds will have a field day.

On the other hand, the disadvantage of digging is that if the topsoil is not very deep the sterile subsoil could be brought up to the surface. Subsoil is very infertile and will produce fewer crops.

In days gone by, all new ground was 'double dug' in preparation for planting. This involved digging down, not just to the depth of a spade, but to twice that depth. Over many years, any subsoil brought

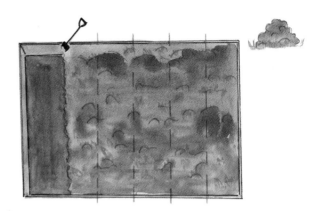

Single digging.

to the surface amalgamated with the topsoil and all the organic matter to create a greater 'depth of topsoil'.

A sensible compromise is to single dig the area to be planted:

- Starting at one end of the bed dig out a spade's depth, known as a 'spit' and put the soil in a wheelbarrow.
- Put this soil in piles at the opposite end of the bed. You may have to pile it on plastic sheeting if there is not enough room.
- Using a fork, turn over the soil at the bottom of the trench. This will loosen and aerate it without the risk of bringing up subsoil.
- Unless you are planning to grow root vegetables in the bed, put in a layer of organic matter along the bottom. (The root vegetable beds will need the addition of organic matter the following year when they are prepared for a different crop – *see* 'Crop Rotation' in Chapter 7.)
- Then start the next row, digging out a spit of soil, turning it and inverting it into the previous trench. In this way, you will ensure that the most fertile surface soil goes to the bottom where the vegetable roots will be and any weeds or dormant seeds will be well buried.
- Leave the soil to settle down for a couple of weeks. Ideally, the digging should be done in the autumn, with the winter weather breaking up the clods of earth before spring.
- Finally, rake it over in early spring, breaking up any clods and removing the remaining weeds.

WORMS

Charles Darwin considered worms to be the most important animals on Earth. They spend their dark lives eating plant debris and defecating as they move through it. The result is that the soil is turned over and aerated constantly and the nutrients are returned to the soil.

There are many different species of worms. Bright red tiger worms live only in the compost heap, munching their way through your plant waste. Other, different species of earthworms live in different types of soil, be it damp and sticky, dry and sandy, or rich with organic matter just beneath the lawn. So don't leap to the conclusion if you don't see the bright red tiger worms from the compost heap wriggling about when you dig, that there aren't any worms in your soil. It's just that your soil has different sorts of worms.

If the beds are raised, the ground at the bottom should be turned over with a fork to improve the drainage before importing topsoil to cover it and fill up the beds. Ensure that you remove or kill off any weeds. They are quite capable of putting on a bit of height and popping their heads up in the spring.

Incorporating organic matter

Everyone knows that the secret of successful vegetable gardening lies in the soil and that the answer to most soil problems is the same: preparing the ground with lots of organic matter. In rural areas this can take the form of animal manure delivered from your handy neighbouring stables or farm. Ensure that it is either already at least a year old, or be prepared to keep it for another season. Steaming, fresh manure can rob the soil of its nutrients and burn the roots and stems of plants and vegetables unfortunate enough to come into contact with it.

But most of us are urban gardeners. So a compost heap becomes an essential part of growing vegetables and flowers. Put simply, you are returning the rotted-down leaves, flowers, stems and roots, with all their nutrients, back to the soil they grew out of. Adding in vegetable waste from the kitchen, grass cuttings full of nitrogen and tea leaves and coffee grounds increases the nutrients for your vegetables. Compost heaps and their maintenance are explored in detail in Chapter 10.

Organic matter (OM), be it manure or garden compost, has a remarkable effect on the texture of any soil. If your soil is sandy and free-draining your vegetables will almost certainly suffer from drought at some point in the summer. Organic matter will hold the moisture like a sponge for as long as it is present. On heavy, clay soil that is hard to dig when it is wet or very dry, OM will break it up so that excess moisture can drain away and it will remain open and damp for longer in dry spells. On ordinary soils that are neither free-draining sand nor sticky clay, OM will simply improve the texture and introduce worms and other organisms to keep the soil in good heart.

Not all vegetables require OM immediately prior to sowing, so the whole area will not need to be treated at the same time. Leafy vegetables prefer the OM to be incorporated in the autumn before spring sowing. (Although you could simply fork it over the ground in autumn and let the worms turn it into the soil during the winter; the ground would then only need to be lightly forked over in spring prior to sowing.) Peas, beans, courgettes and so on prefer to grow into the soil above a trench or a hole full of OM. Root vegetables are best grown on ground that was manured the previous year.

Preparing the ground for sowing

If you have succeeded in weedkilling and digging over the beds before Christmas, then the winter rains and frost will get into the clods of earth and break them up rather like ice cracks unlagged pipes. In the spring, therefore, rake the surface soil down to what the old gardeners called a 'fine tilth': that is, until the soil resembles breadcrumbs. Any stones and bits of weed should be removed.

If you have started preparing the ground in the spring it will be necessary to break down the big lumps of soil and then create a fine tilth. The result will be a 'fluffy' soil that is full of air pockets. It will eventually settle down, but you can speed the process. Starting in one corner, shuffle your feet in a straight line to the opposite corner. Turn around and shuffle back. And so on, backwards and forwards, until the whole bed has been gently trampled. Rake it over lightly to finish it off and the soil is ready for sowing and planting.

STALE SEEDBED TECHNIQUE

On newly turned ground it's a good idea to get rid of the dormant seeds from lower levels of the soil.

- Fork the surface over to lift the dormant weed seeds nearer the surface so that they can germinate.
- A few weeks later, hoe the seedlings off.
- Wait until a second and third flush of weed seedlings have germinated and been hoed off.
- Finally, rake the soil and sow or plant the young vegetables.

CHAPTER 6

Decorative elements

Once the design of the layout has been settled upon, the paths and edgings put in and the ground made ready for planting, it's time to take a look at some of the colours, textures, planting combinations and finishing touches for the potager. These are the elements that lift a purely practical vegetable garden into the realms of artful decoration.

A 'cake-slice' bed in the semicircular potager.

PATTERN

Dividing the overall area into a regular pattern of beds allows the opportunity to repeat and contrast that pattern within the beds themselves. In a grid of square and rectangular beds it works well to think in terms of symmetry. If one bed of a symmetrical pair has parallel lines across the bed, then the other bed looks better if its lines run the same way. The neighbouring beds could be planted in lines along the bed, at right angles to the previous ones. And so on.

However, quite often, by the end of the season the symmetry, if not the geometry, gets a bit lost under a welter of leaves and flowers. But order is restored as each line of vegetables is finished and cleared away and another sowing is made in a neat, straight line.

In circular and semicircular potagers, however, it is a little more difficult. The easiest and most successful method is to divide the plot into 'cake slices'. However, there is an integral problem: each slice ends in a point. This leads the way to planting in groups rather than lines. If the shape of each section is emphasized with edging, the design is underscored and its strength carries the less formal planting. The total effect is of an open brocade skirt with different textures, forms and colours.

SCALE

In the large potager garden at the Château of Villandry in France, each bed holds a single variety of vegetable or flower. On such a large scale, the beds become elements in an overall pattern, which is intended to be seen from the living apartments of the owners of the château. The gardens are

Each bed is an element in the overall design at Villandry.

A grid pattern of rectangular beds (RHS Chelsea Flower Show, 2008).

entirely ornamental: the vegetables are not picked and eaten. To do so would break up the design.

In the show garden at the Chelsea Flower Show in 2008 illustrated on page 65, each 1m (39in) square bed contains just one variety of lettuce, cabbage or ruby chard, with just the occasional perennial thyme edging for effect. The grid pattern is emphasized by the wickerwork edgers. The different foliage textures contrast each square against its neighbour, while colour is simply added in the form of the dark purple lavender, *L*. 'Hidcote'.

From a practical point of view, the constraint of this pattern would again be that it would spoil the design to cut individual cabbages or lettuces from the beds. But most are filled with herbs and others with salads and chard whose leaves are picked and the remainder left to regrow. So if the type of vegetable that is harvested a little at a time were to be grown, this design would be practical. Sprouts, sprouting broccoli, peas and beans would all lend themselves to these plantings. And if some of the beds were filled with flowers, such as the white borage in the background, the overall effect would be strong and extremely attractive.

The monochrome beauty of winter in a formal vegetable garden.

The paths between the beds have been minimized for display purposes. Clearly, if the layout were to be copied at least some of the paths in between would need to be made wider for reasons of practical access. The wickerwork edgers would also need to be renewed every three or four years.

In a small garden, the elements of pattern and colour can be contained within the individual beds. If the balance between ornament and practicality is tipped more towards growing and harvesting vegetables, it makes sense to grow different vegetables and flowers in the same bed, so that whenever a cabbage is picked, for example, the remaining elements in the bed distract attention away from the gap.

COLOUR

In winter, the skeleton of a strictly formal structure – the paths, edges, evergreen planting and ornamentation – create an overall pattern in monochrome that is sparse, elegant and essentially pleasing. In spring, summer and autumn the changing patterns of the vegetables and flowers clothe the skeleton with colour, form and texture.

Different elements within a single bed.

Summer colours.

Whenever you step into any garden it is partly the use of colour that dictates the mood and atmosphere you experience. Vegetable gardens are no different. In all probability, the feeling that will be engendered is one of vibrant generosity, rather than calm restfulness. And strong, hot colours create a positive mood.

But if you were to create a corner of the potager where you might want to sit and have a cup of tea, the colour temperature could be lowered to cooler pastels and herbs could be grown for their scent.

The pinks and purple of scented geraniums and Heliotrope Cherry Pie invite you to pause.

Both the gentle pastel shades and wafting perfume invite you to linger for a while. An apple tree might create a little shade.

Blues, mauves and pinks retreat away from you into the distance. Think of the view from a mountain top. As the hills in the distance recede from your gaze they appear to become increasingly blue and mauve. They are passive colours that melt into a background. Consequently, they make a small area seem larger.

Whites, reds and yellows are strong colours that appear to advance towards your eye. They are full of energy; they hold your attention. If you watch a dramatic winter sunset, how often do you turn around to look at the approaching darkness to the east? Strong colours demand positive action and reaction. Red apples are ripe and ready to be picked and eaten. Orange beetles are flashing a warning to their prospective predators: leave us alone, we are highly poisonous.

In every garden, the colours vary with the seasons. They change as crops are sown, then grow; produce flowers or fruits and are harvested. All except the colour green: green is the universal backdrop to our gardens. Everything that is grown

Red and green lettuces.

is either in harmony or in contrast with the colour of the grass, the trees and the leaves.

It is worth taking some time to study the principles of the 'colour wheel'. Opposite green on the colour wheel is red. Red creates a strong contrast to green, while the colours closest to green combine

Mauve catmint and dark red nasturtiums.

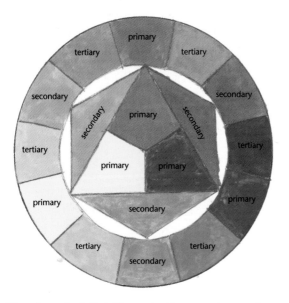

The colour wheel. Red, blue and yellow are primary colours. Green, orange and violet are secondary colours made by mixing neighbouring primaries. The other colours link the primaries to the secondaries.

Autumn reds and purples.

harmoniously. Adding a touch of contrasting colour to a harmonious combination sparks it into life; adding a few dark harmonious colours calms down a riot of strong tones.

In the natural world, colours are not flat monotones. They are shaded. So sometimes colour

Beetroot leaves like stained glass.

Glossy leaves and boot-black shining seedcases on annual Hibiscus.

combinations work better, or worse, than you might expect. As the plants grow from seedlings into mature plants, their foliage darkens. It is often enriched with natural hormonal colours such as anthocyanin, which lends red and purple tones to leaves, stems, fruit and flowers, and flavin, which is yellow.

The intensity of light changes with the seasons as the sun climbs in the sky. In spring, the light is gentle and pale, so colours are watery and subtle. Pale green seedlings, leaf buds and new grass contrast with a few bright crocus and tulips. Gradually, the light grows in intensity, until at midsummer the sun is at its brightest and colours are therefore at their strongest. But as the summer wears into autumn the colours mellow and deepen. The green chlorophyll in the leaves is broken down, giving way to the reds and yellows of anthocyanins and flavins. By December and January, the light is at its weakest and the sun at its lowest in the sky, so colours are at their palest.

TEXTURE

As light falls on the surface of textured leaves it changes the colours. When the sun glances across the surface of a crumpled red leaf it becomes a kaleidoscope of colour and light.

Purple leaves in shade become visual holes.

Red cabbages and beetroot leaves with the light behind them are as brilliant as stained glass in the sun after a shower. Orange marigolds and red *Amaranthus* (Love Lies Bleeding) heat up the action even on a dull day. But when red- and purple-leaved plants are shaded they disappear, creating visual holes in the design.

Contrasting the leaf textures is just as effective in the vegetable garden as it is in the herbaceous border. Cabbages have a silvery bloom like ripe plums that is damaged with just the touch of a finger. Contrast that with the feathery foliage of carrots and fennel, or the downy flowers, stems and leaves of borage. Then add in the textures of flowers

The hairy down of white borage.

Contrasting textures and forms.

The green-bloomed dome of winter cabbage.

and their foliage and the potager beds are at least as visually rich and varied as any garden border.

SHAPE AND FORM

Just as colours and textures add depth to the pattern of vegetables and flowers, so do the shapes and forms of the stems, leaves and flowers. The cut leaves of globe artichokes arise early in the spring. As a permanent plant, globe artichokes prefer a dry, sunny position, as do tulips. Their beautiful silver foliage is strong enough in shape and form to contrast with classic round and pointed tulips. Then, as the tulip leaves die back and are cleared away, the ground becomes dry enough for the bulbs to survive without the need to dig them up. As the globe artichokes extend their dramatic buds and flowers skywards, the leaves become very large and would swamp anything in their vicinity. So give them the run of a perennial bed, or plant them along a tall boundary fence or wall.

The different textures and colours of lettuces are decorative right from the first plantings in spring and throughout the season. They would liven up a line of longer-term winter vegetables with much duller leaves, and once the lettuces are all picked those vegetables would have more room to expand and develop.

A bed of green-domed winter cabbages forming a grid pattern is artistic in autumn just as it stands. And as the surrounding beds are cleared and forked over, the uniform globes of the cabbages in a regular pattern make an abstract pattern against the dark brown soil.

Height and verticality can be achieved not just with globe artichokes and wigwams of beans, but with rows of sunflowers, Jerusalem artichokes and squashes trained along a fence. Even pumpkins can be trained up a post if they are small.

Contrasts of shape, colour and texture.

(left) Orange spheres of small pumpkins have been trained up a post to illuminate the autumn bed like an abstract lighting system.

Upright sword shapes of sweetcorn plants provide a strong vertical accent to any combination of flowers and foliage. The crumpled mounds of large-leaved Swiss chard and the flat plates of the nasturtiums contrast well. Add in some splashes of dark red *Amaranthus* and this combination is strong and eye-catching.

Ranks of erect leeks marching across a bed like soldiers are emphatically straight against the horizontal planes of the path. The busby of blue-green leaves tops them off. Add in a few companion French marigolds and intercropping alfafa and the effect is not lost but heightened.

Nasturtiums spill out over the wicker edges.

Low-growing French marigolds make an eye-catching corner plant. And nasturtiums, despite their propensity to attract blackfly, spill out over paths and edgers very romantically.

The joy of making plant combinations in the vegetable garden is that it is all so ephemeral. Next season presents a blank canvas to attempt new combinations and re-use old favourites.

ARCHES, TUNNELS AND PERGOLAS

Ornamental vegetable gardens do not need to be enclosed potagers. They form a part of the garden as a whole. They may even be the entire garden: they deserve centre stage.

But, if the potager is enclosed and separated, the entrance becomes more important. It marks the

Vertical ranks of leeks.

The entrance to the potager from the garden.

transition from the outer, ornamental garden into a different space. Few gardeners have the luxury of an old walled kitchen garden; few of us would have the time and energy to tend it, either. But the image of a wooden door in a high wall concealing the inner garden like the lid on a jewellery box is there in the subconscious. And it inspires the need to formalize the entrance, whether there is a wall there or not.

An archway signals an entrance effectively. It is visible from elsewhere in the wider garden. It invites you in. Another arch repeated further into the garden, or down the main axial path, draws you through the beds.

The materials should be in harmony. If there is one forged metal arch, then all the other structures, if possible, should also be made of the same forged metal. Using the same materials throughout the garden draws it together. If one arch were made of forged metal, the next of bamboos and a third of wood, the garden becomes 'bitty'. It lacks cohesion.

Forged metal is expensive, but at the other end of the scale woven hazel branches or willow are cheap, or could even be homemade. These also have the advantage of being short-lived, so that a few years later everything could be changed around. However, if your garden is prone to gusty winds and the arch has become top-heavy with the weight of runner beans or apples, it is liable to topple.

Arches made of treated timber are also less expensive than forged metal. The wood is usually guaranteed rot-proof for a period of ten years, but in twenty it will start to show its age and will

Worked metal arch.

probably need replacing. Wooden arches also become vulnerable to strong winds however well the uprights have been concreted in.

Permanent living arches of apple or pear are another alternative. They use the available space productively and can be pruned easily. Choose a pair of cordon apples or pears that are trained to single stems. Buy 'whips' that are young and flexible so that you can bend the main stems to shape and tie them to a supporting structure. Once the young whips have made strong curving trunks the frame can be removed.

Arches could, of course, be extended into tunnels, which are ideal for supporting all sorts of climbers, from trained apples and pears, to runner beans and

Vine-covered trelliswork arch.

An informal woven hazel arch supports a crop of dwarf squashes.

sweet peas. If the tunnel is to be permanent make sure it is wide enough to allow for growth within and for you and your wheelbarrow to get through on a rainy afternoon.

Less permanent tunnels of cut willow or hazel are equally useful, if short-lived. Wooden tunnels are longer lasting, but they too have a limited life: dark, dank wooden tunnels perhaps more so than just an archway.

Where paths cross is an ideal location for erecting a pergola. It signals the meeting of the ways and possibly the centre of the whole garden. A pergola also makes an excellent climbing frame, as well as an excuse for growing less practical plants. You would be justified in planting scented flowers that attract pollinating insects.

Wisteria could be trained into the pergola in southern counties of the UK. As a climber against

---

SCENTED CLIMBERS FOR A PERGOLA

Roses and summer jasmine would all grow well in most areas of the UK. *Rosa* 'Zephyrine Drouhin' has large, perfumed, bright pink flowers on completely thornless stems. It usually repeats later in the summer after a June flowering. Tie the new growth down horizontally in spring to the framework of the pergola and the stems will 'break' into flower.

Summer jasmine is tough and would need to be tidied up, cut back and tied into the framework in spring, or it might get tangled and too woody. Alternatively, in warmer areas of the country you could use *Trachelospermum jasminoides*. It's similar to, but much less vigorous than, summer jasmine. It's evergreen and has sweetly scented white flowers all summer.

---

a house wall its flowers are perfectly frost-hardy, but a free-standing pergola does not offer the same frost protection as a house wall. Tie the young growth into the framework of the pergola in the first year or two. Try not to let it twist itself around the uprights. Eventually they will be the size and strength of wooden pythons and could seriously distort the metalwork. Side shoots should be shortened by half their length in August and cut back to two or three buds from the main stem in January. These 'spurs' will then flower the following year.

If a fence encloses the potager from the garden it can be used as protection against rabbits. They are a growing problem in country gardens. A rabbit-proof fence can be incorporated either when the fence is erected, or afterwards (*see* Chapter 4). A smart paling fence surrounding neat rows of vegetables has a 'Peter Rabbit' effect. It looks right, more so than a more reliably rabbit-proof larch-lap fence. If it is painted white it can suddenly look rather 'colonial American', although this may look a little out of place in the UK.

Wisterias cover a central pergola.

A ripening squash on its own shelf.

However, even a low, 1m (39in) fence can be used to support all the usual climbers, including sweet peas and cradles of pumpkins and squashes. If it's a little taller you could train cultivated blackberries along it or a delicious loganberry. They would be highly decorative as well as productive.

FINISHING TOUCHES

The centre of a symmetrical potager demands attention. This is the focus and focal point of the garden. Filling it with cabbages or marigolds somehow fails to excite.

At Villandry there are dipping ponds at the centre of each quadrant. Installing the water pipe and pump at the outset is just a routine job; trying to put it in at a later date is too disruptive of paths, edges and beds. A pond that has a constant water supply, an overflow and pump would be very useful in summer, but you would have to bend down and lift out countless full watering cans to water the beds. So it might be better to install an entire irrigation system at the building stage.

A bay tree is traditionally grown at the centre of a formal vegetable or herb garden. It is usually trained into a cone or a ball on a stem and looks elegant even in winter. However, bay trees come

A trained bay tree makes an elegant centrepiece.

from southern Europe, so they like sunshine and a draining soil, and they are a little vulnerable to a windy or cold site. Trim them to shape every April and at the same time give them a small feed that is high in nitrogen.

Single wooden posts are ideal to train the occasional mini-pumpkin skywards, but there are ornamental posts available that are much more interesting.

Just a single ironwork spiral is often sufficient to support a young apple tree, a cloud of sweet peas, or a single sunflower. A row of twisting uprights finished off with a finial would support a row of climbing peas beautifully. They are works of art in their own right. These too can be moved around the garden as and where they are needed, or they can be fixed permanently at strategic positions in the beds.

Ironwork birds and animals also lend a sense of humour to the more serious business of tending the potager's vegetables.

Ironwork chickens beneath the bay tree.

Ironwork spiral.

Adding a touch of humour.

CHAPTER 7

Planning the sowing and growing

As soon as the soil has been prepared it's time to get sowing and growing. But first it pays to think ahead. It's sensible to sow little and often to avoid gluts. There are only so many lettuces, cabbages and courgettes that you and yours can eat at any one time. An ornamental vegetable garden makes this principle much easier to follow, as it is designed to have smaller beds.

Ornamental vegetable gardens are designed to have smaller beds.

CROP ROTATION

In any vegetable garden, of whatever size, it makes sense to change what you grow each year in any one space. If you keep growing cabbages, for example, in the same soil year after year you will gradually build up all sorts of undesirable pests and diseases. Anything from root aphids to club root disease remains in the soil waiting to affect each crop. Soil nutrients are used in different amounts by different

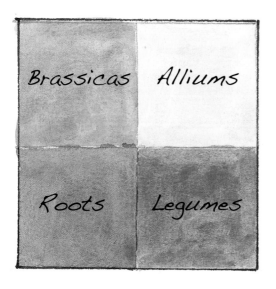

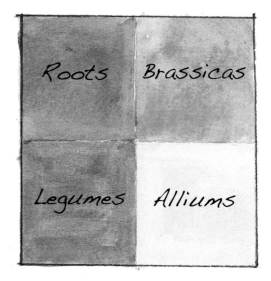

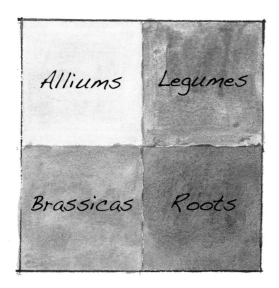

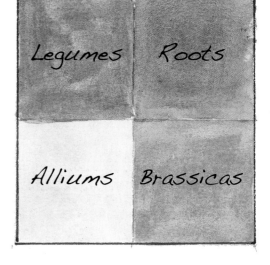

Four-year crop rotation.

crops, so however much fertilizer and organic matter you use some nutrients will be used up completely each year, while others will remain unused and build up in the soil.

To overcome these problems crop rotation is the answer: that is, growing different sorts of vegetables each season in each bed. In this way, they will use up different nutrients and any pests or diseases one crop leaves in the soil are less likely to affect the next crop.

Vegetables are generally classified into the following types:

- brassicas: cabbages, broccoli, Brussels sprouts, kale
- legumes and marrows: peas and beans, courgettes, pumpkins and squashes
- root crops: beetroot, carrot, parsnip, swede and so on
- alliums: the entire onion family including leeks
- potatoes (optional in the rotation)

Note that if you plan to grow perennial vegetables and fruit, they will take up a permanent space in the garden.

The first three groups include most, but not all, the vegetables you will be growing. Others that do not fit easily into any of these groups, such as sweetcorn or outdoor tomatoes, can be placed with the legumes and marrows group.

Members of the onion family are less fussy about growing in the same place twice, but it's probably wise on balance to move them around if room can be found. Certainly any sign of fungal rust or neck rot should prompt you to move them on the following year.

Potatoes carry the risk of potato blight, a devastating disease that partly caused the famine in Ireland in the nineteenth century. Once a crop has been blighted the ground should not be used again for growing potatoes, or outdoor tomatoes, for a minimum of seven years. The same is true for potato eelworm, which makes scabs on the skins. The eelworm eggs remain dormant in the soil for years, so it's essential that you move the potatoes around each year. Eelworm does not affect tomatoes. The alternative to growing them in the ground is to grow them in 20ltr (35pt) pots of proprietary compost well away from any tomatoes you may also be growing. Blight can be transmitted from the potatoes to the tomatoes.

Each of the main three groups requires different soil preparation each year. So there is a natural succession:

- In Year One, the ground is prepared for the brassicas by incorporating organic matter into the soil in the autumn, allowing the winter to break it all down. Organic fertilizer is raked in before sowing.
- In the following Year Two, the ground is just raked over with no addition of organic matter or fertilizer and the root crops are sown. (If the land is fertilized or manured the roots will fork as they go off in different directions seeking the nutrients.)
- In Year Three, organic matter and fertilizer are dug in immediately prior to sowing or planting legumes and marrows.
- In Year Four, the ground should be improved with organic matter during the autumn for planting onions and their kin in the spring.

Beds for perennial planting should also be improved with organic matter in the autumn and planted during the winter and spring. Add a mulch of compost or well-rotted manure every following winter.

Make a working plan of the beds and write in each what you are going to grow, bearing in mind the principles of crop rotation. It's easy the first year. The second and third years you may find slightly more problematic and a compromise will have to be achieved. But the more you rotate the crops, the fewer will be the problems and the better the health of the vegetables.

SEED STORAGE

It pays to buy good-quality seed, preferably during the preceding winter so that it can be stored correctly. When the seed packets arrive, or when you bring them home from the garden centre, put them in a sealed plastic box in the fridge. This will keep the seed at a constant temperature of about 4–5°C

(39–41°F). The humidity will also be constant. In this way, any seed can be stored for up to six months. Thereafter it does depend on what the seed is. As a rule of thumb, the finer the seed the longer it remains viable. Some vegetable seed such as lettuce has to be stored at a low temperature. If you leave lettuce seed in the garden shed on a sunny day the high temperatures will cause a heat-induced dormancy and the lettuce seed will germinate irregularly.

Keeping unused seed from one year to the next is not really worthwhile. Its viability will probably decline and you will have gone to all the trouble and time of raising the seed, likely with little success. For what it produces, vegetable seed is very good value. It's well worth buying fresh seed each year.

Saving your own seed

The cost of seed does increase year on year, although a lot of work goes into collecting, transporting and packaging that seed. If you are happy with the quality of your beans or peas, you could leave a few pods to mature on the plants. Pick them on a sunny afternoon when they are ripe and leave the pods to dry in a frost-free shed or garage. Once they have dried out to a crisp you can extract the seeds, discarding any that are shrivelled or mouldy and put them in a paper envelope. Mark the envelope and store it over the winter in a plastic box in the fridge.

However, many vegetables are biennial: that is, they only flower and set seed in the second summer. Leeks, cabbages, carrots, to name but a few, will need to be left to flower *in situ*, taking up space that is probably better used by another crop.

Some seed is marked 'F¹ hybrid'. This means, in short, that it will not produce the same top-quality crop from its own seeds. Although this seed is more expensive, it is not worth saving it: F¹ hybrids do not come 'true' from seed. The vegetables they produce are always inferior.

Rows of seedling kale between young lettuces.

SOWING

The general principle of sowing little and often is particularly true of crops that are best eaten immediately they are picked. These include lettuces, radishes, summer spinach, French beans and peas. Packets of mixed salad leaves are useful because the different elements mature at different times over a longer season. Cut-and-come-again lettuces are equally good value: they are slow to bolt and you can pick their leaves for weeks.

All seed should be sown thinly, as this will allow it to grow away more quickly and the seedlings will be healthier. They will also take greater advantage of the water and nutrients available in the soil.

The same factors apply to thinning the seedlings once they have germinated. If they are overcrowded for too long they will be vulnerable to fungal diseases. They will grow tall and leggy in their search for light and the resulting plants will grow more slowly and sickly. Tender, sweet vegetables depend on rapid growth.

Timing

As soon as you see a faint green haze on the hedgerows, the garden weeds are just beginning to germinate and the buds on the trees are beginning to swell, you can be quite sure that spring has sprung. Everything is responding to the rising soil temperature as well as the increase in day length. (The soil needs to be about 10°C (50°F) for most seed to germinate.)

It's important to sow at the correct time. Seed that is sown too early does not germinate, because the soil is too cold: it rots, especially if the soil is wet. A lot of seed can be sown as soon as the first signs of spring are apparent. However, some seed – courgettes and runner beans for instance – will produce seedlings that are not frost-hardy, so they will need to be sown later. And other seed needs to be sown later in the summer to produce a crop in the autumn, or the following spring.

Making drills

The ground should have been raked to a fine tilth beforehand and left to settle for a few days. In the

Young runner beans, lettuces and leeks in May.

small sections of an ornamental vegetable garden there is no need to tread on the beds, but, if it seems necessary, put down a plank to walk on rather than tread on the raked soil.

- Use pegs and a line as a guide.
- Draw the corner of the rake along the straight line, creating a shallow depression.
- Sow the seed thinly along the depression.
- Rake the soil back gently.
- Stand the rake upright and lightly tamp down the soil along the row.
- Mark each end of the row with a stick and label it with the name and date sown.

Sowing in the greenhouse

If you have a greenhouse, whether it is heated or cold, you can steal a march on the season by sowing into plugs and pots. Most seed will germinate quickly, often within a week, depending on the conditions and the seed. So it's important to plan ahead. Once pairs of true leaves are visible, the seedlings should be pricked out or transplanted into larger containers of all-purpose compost, or an organic equivalent. Plan ahead: they will use up more space in pots than in seed trays.

The greenhouse in late spring. Tomatoes, aubergines and peppers are growing away in small pots, while containers of summer bedding plants are waiting to go out.

Some young plants can be hardened off and planted out. Others will need frost protection so sowing should be delayed until April so that by the time they are ready to leave their pots the nights will be warmer.

In general the quicker the young plants are moved on, the sturdier they will grow. If they are left struggling in too small a container for too long they will become weak, leggy and malnourished, and they will produce poor results.

The regime and needs of each vegetable are described under each heading in Chapter 8.

BUYING YOUNG PLANTS

Young vegetable plants are often available in farmers' markets and at the garden centre. They are particularly useful if you have no greenhouse or space available in which to raise your own plants. Buy them little and often, and plant them up straight away. Sometimes you will find that they have been in their containers rather too long. Buy only bright green plants with the roots just showing at the bottom of the plugs or containers. Ignore cabbage seedlings with purplish leaves (unless they are red cabbages, of course); put back peas or beans that have long, trailing white roots coming out of the bottom, or, worse still, dead brown ones; and leave behind tall, gangly young tomatoes with long spaces between the leaf joints. None of these will produce good vegetables – they have been in their containers for too long. Vegetables growing in pots have a very short shelf life.

Thinning and hardening off

Seed that has been sown directly in the outdoor beds will need thinning to the distances recommended on the seed packet. Wait until the seedlings have made at least their first pair of leaves, then remove the weakest. It's a good time to do a little hand-weeding too. Now that the rows of seedlings are easily seen it's also a chance to hoe between them. Once the seedlings have got their spaces to themselves they will quickly grow away without competition from their peers and the weeds.

Plants that have been raised in the greenhouse should be ready to be hardened off from the end of April. If they are left indoors too long they will outgrow their pots and become weak and starved of nutrients. Move the pots into a cold frame, or place them in a sheltered spot near the greenhouse. If a frost is forecast, cover the cold frames at night to protect the young plants within. Those that are standing outside would need to be brought back into the greenhouse for protection. It will be safe to plant out the young vegetables permanently once the frosts are finished. Timing it right can be quite tricky. Check the length of germination times before you sow indoors and work it out backwards (*see* Chapter 8 for details of the individual vegetables).

PLANTING OUT

Use a stake and line to make a straight line if necessary on the prepared bed. Next, pop in the individual plants with a hand trowel; firm them in with your hands (not your boot); water them well; and mark the row with the label from the batch of plants. At this stage, cabbage seedlings look exactly the same as sprouts or broccoli, while young marrows, courgettes and pumpkins are also easily confused.

Cabbages, sprouts or broccoli will need protection from birds, cabbage white butterflies and, in country areas, rabbits. (Chapter 10 covers organic methods and companion planting as ways to protect your crops.)

Runner beans, as well as some peas and French beans, will need supports when they are planted out. In an ornamental vegetable garden, wigwams are perhaps the easiest on the eye. These are simple to construct, with canes pushed down well into the ground at intervals of about 30cm (12in) in a circle. Make the circle as big as you can accommodate.

Tie the tops together with string. Plant the peas or beans, one either side of each cane.

There are also permanent supports and ornamental wigwams available made of forged metal, or, less permanently, of hazel. If these are sourced locally they will have a considerably lower carbon footprint than bamboo canes.

Alternatively, the traditional row of beans is just as easy to make. The intervals can be greater between the individual canes, which gives the beans a bit more space at the roots and less competition for moisture.

Perhaps the crows are scared . . .

A hazel wigwam.

A ballcock ensures that the large bucket is kept constantly full. Water is fed from the large tank above that collects rainwater off the house and garage roofs.

WATERING THE VEGETABLES

Some vegetables need more water at certain stages of their development than others.
    It pays to prioritize if there are water shortages.

- Aim to keep vegetables with a high water content irrigated daily in dry weather. These include courgettes, pumpkins and squashes, lettuce, spinach, sweetcorn, tomatoes, cucumbers and most greenhouse crops.
- As peas and beans start to develop their pods, they also need plenty of moisture. Spray over the flowers too with a hose. In sunny weather this helps the flowers to 'set', or turn into beans.
- Newly planted and young vegetables whose root systems have not got down far into the soil should also be watered. Don't water them little and often, though, or the roots will remain just beneath the surface relying on your regular sprinkles to keep them going. It's better to give them a thorough dowsing every few days to encourage those roots to go down to lower, damper levels.

It's useful to have plenty of water butts if there is a drought. Buy them in advance: they become like hen's teeth once the word 'drought' is mentioned in the media. Rainwater can be collected from the house roof and the greenhouse and shed roofs too. If you are a little ingenious you could feed the water from the butt or tank through a hose into a container in the greenhouse, or somewhere handy. If a plumber's ballcock is installed, the container will be kept constantly filled and ready for use.

SUCCESSION PLANTING

Space is precious in the small beds of an ornamental vegetable garden. It becomes important to use every square inch of soil productively. As one vegetable has finished being harvested and is cleared away, the space left can be used immediately by the next crop. This could be more of the same to keep up a continuity of supply, or it may be something entirely different. With careful planning you can take advantage of the vacant spaces.

The most important factor is to keep the soil in good health. Organic matter added at the correct time, and maybe the addition of compost tea to improve the population of beneficial organisms below ground, will ensure that your vegetables will succeed and not grow hungry (*see* Chapter 10).

It's also important to take into account the order of crop rotation if at all possible. This will ensure that different nutrients are being used by different vegetables and that specific pests and fungal diseases are not built up in the soil (*see* above). As soon as one crop has finished, remove the debris and add it to the compost heap. Weed the soil: inevitably volunteers will have insinuated themselves in between the vegetable plants however well you have been weeding. Rake it over and you are ready to fill the gap:

- As soon as the overwintered vegetables such as broccoli, sprouts and leeks have finished and been removed, the space could be occupied by peas, beans, courgettes and pumpkins.
- Once the broad beans have finished, cut off the tops and plant a leafy vegetable such as winter cabbage alongside to make use of the nitrogen left in the soil by the beans.
- As the summer crops are removed, follow them up with late sowings of perpetual spinach in August and September, or late-sown round peas in October and November to crop the following May and June (*see* Chapter 8).
- Japanese onions can be sown in August to crop the following year.
- Aquadulce longpod broad beans and garlic could be sown in November after the summer crops have been cleared away in the autumn.
- Successional sowings of summer vegetables also find a place in the vacated spaces of earlier crops. Peas, French beans, carrots and the usual salads such as lettuce, radish and rocket could all be sown at intervals of two or three weeks. Sow them little and often so that you avoid a glut (*see* Appendix).

And of course in an ornamental vegetable garden, flowers can be used to fill the spaces:

- Dahlias could be planted out in late May after the winter vegetables and the frosts are over. Prepare the ground thoroughly with lots more organic matter and water them in thoroughly.
- If annuals are sown in plugs and pots, they can take their place as young plants only a step away from flowering in early summer. For example, once the leeks are out of the ground by April the space could be occupied with hardy annuals for the remainder of the summer. And autumn-sown peas could replace the annuals as they fade.

INTERCROPPING

Vegetable plants grow at different rates: some occupy a space for almost an entire calendar year, while others are much faster to grow and harvest. So it makes sense to use the spare soil between crops that are slower to develop.

Rows of cabbages, sprouts and broccoli that have been sown or planted out in spring will have plenty

An intercrop of fast-growing lettuces between rows of longer-term chard and kale.

of room to accommodate a quick crop of French beans. Sow the beans in March in the greenhouse to steal a few weeks from the timetable and they will be ready to plant out in May. By the time the brassicas need space to spread their leaves the beans will be finished. Cut the beans down, leaving the roots, which will mean that those nitrogen-forming root nodules will be on hand to give the brassicas a nitrogenous midsummer boost.

Similarly, a sowing of lettuces, radishes or rocket could be made between some of the slow-growing root vegetables such as parsnips. Take care, however, not to add the customary organic matter or fertilizer for the salads, or the parsnips may make forked roots.

Rows of lettuces and salad leaves are in the path of the courgette in the background. The lettuces will have been picked and eaten by the time the courgette leaves swamp their space.

CHAPTER 8

What to grow – vegetables

Transplanting seedlings in the greenhouse.

It's an exciting moment when the seed catalogues come plopping through the letterbox in the early spring. Every page seems to list so very many varieties of every vegetable you have ever met and some you never knew existed. There are some that no supermarket ever stocks. Salsify, for example, is rightly called 'the vegetable oyster' for its delicious, subtle flavour. But it's quite long-winded to prepare for the pot and few shoppers would buy it more than once. It also has a very short shelf life.

Some quite ordinary vegetables feature in large numbers in the catalogues. Potato varieties, for example, are many and various, ranging from the usual old favourites to those with purple-coloured flesh and the French chefs' favourite, 'Ratte'. This main crop potato has dense, waxy flesh, just like the tastiest new potato you've ever eaten. They are well worth growing even in the smallest garden, perhaps planted in a 20ltr (35pt) container.

Most vegetables when prepared and cooked within minutes of being picked have a quite different flavour. Anyone who has tried the sweet, nutty flavour of freshly picked, button-sized sprouts will never again go near the sulphuric old bombs that are sold in the shops.

So it's well worth finding room for quite humble vegetables in your ornamental plot. Others, however, are better left out. Cauliflowers, for example, are notoriously difficult to grow. They deeply resent root disturbance from transplanting or hoeing and if they are unhappy they tend to make very small curds that quickly bolt, or run to flower. Even if you do achieve a good head, it will prove to be wriggling with little green caterpillars unless you have doused it with pesticides at frequent intervals. Celeriac, that darling of the cookery shows, rarely produces anything much bigger than a golf ball in this country.

Most types of celery have to be blanched by tying up the stems with black plastic, resulting in a slimy, wet slug bonanza. And even self-blanching celery is usually sticky with the grey molluscs.

Research and development of better vegetable varieties is constantly improving and changing what can be grown successfully by the amateur in the UK. Twenty years ago, it would have been almost impossible to grow aubergines of any size even in a heated greenhouse. Now there are modern varieties that grow better in lower temperatures in our short British summers; they also seem more resistant to the whitefly that beset aubergine plants from the seedling stage. Carrots have been bred over the past few years that do not attract carrot root fly. They are just as sweet and tasty as the others, but without the tunnels full of little grey maggots that are so dispiriting and disgusting.

THE MAIN NUTRIENTS NEEDED BY ALL VEGETABLES

The major nutrients – NPK – are essential for healthy plant growth:

- Nitrogen (N) encourages vegetative growth: green leaves and shoots.
- Phosphorous (P) is vital for seed germination and root growth and it helps ripen the fruit.
- Potassium (K) encourages hard growth that is resistant to disease and frost. It is needed for the production of flowers and fruit: hence tomato fertilizer is high in potassium.

Lesser nutrients have important roles to play too:

- Calcium (Ca) is a constituent of the walls of a plant's cells and in the growing tip of the plant's roots. The high levels of calcium that occur in chalky and limestone soils cause deficiencies in iron, potassium, aluminium and magnesium.
- Magnesium (Mg), moves phosphorous around the plant and is present in the plant's enzymes.
- Iron (Fe) aids the synthesis of chlorophyll in the plant: it helps to make leaves green. A lack of iron, which is often the result of high levels of calcium, is visible in the leaves as yellowing between the veins.

Trace elements are also essential in very small amounts; these are usually present in soils and proprietary composts anyway.

And vegetable breeders are aware of the demand for flavour. One of the great success stories is the rise and rise in popularity of the sweet mini-tomatoes such as 'Gardeners' Delight'. A pot of these on the garden table is an invitation to pick and pop in the mouth, just like a bowl of sweets.

The varieties listed below are especially suitable for the ornamental vegetable garden. Those selected are attractively coloured; smaller growing; resistant to the most common pests; or all of those things. So when it comes to choosing what vegetable seed to order, be a little adventurous. You could grow just a few of any new variety to try it out. You never know, it may prove so popular that every member of the family demands more next year.

VEGETABLE VARIETIES TO GROW OUTDOORS

Brassicas and leafy vegetables

Members of the cabbage family (the brassicas) are many and various. They all prefer an alkaline soil, so if you garden in acid conditions it's worthwhile adding some garden lime at the rate indicated on the packet. Never add lime at the same time as organic matter.

Brassicas like plenty of organic matter to support their fleshy leaves, so add plenty during the autumn prior to sowing. They make heartier cabbages and sprouts if the ground is firm around the plants, so don't be too vigorous with the hoe.

This section also includes leafy vegetables such as spinach, spinach beet and Swiss chard. They have similar nutritional needs: large leaves need lots of nitrogen and plenty of moisture.

Common pests and diseases of brassicas and leafy vegetables
All members of the cabbage family are the favourite foods of marauding pigeons, the cabbage white butterfly, which makes highly visible, yellow and black striped caterpillars, and cabbage moth, which makes well-camouflaged green caterpillars. The plants therefore need to be covered with very fine nets that are butterfly-resistant; also make sure that the edges are firmly fixed to the ground to

A box of cabbages takes little space and is very decorative.

prevent the pigeons from ducking underneath. Slugs and snails are also fond of tender young cabbage leaves, so protect them in whatever way you find acceptable.

Club root is a fungal disease that distorts the growing roots, making them thick and knobbly. The plants become stunted and quickly succumb. It is more common on acid soils, so liming the soil in the late winter to reduce the acidity before sowing is one preventative measure; also ensure that the soil is well worked and drains. Once the soil has grown infected plants, the spores remain for years. Be very fussy if you buy brassica plants of any sort: check that they are growing in commercial compost, not that they have been dug out of the ground where they might have become infected. If club root does

manifest itself in your soil, remove and destroy all brassica plants in the area. Other wild members of the brassica family can host the disease, so make sure that you keep the ground clear especially of hairy bittercress and shepherd's purse. And don't plant wallflowers in or near brassicas.

Cabbage root aphids live entirely below ground, just breaking the surface of the soil, where they cling to the main stem. They suck all the life out of the plants, which then look blue, discoloured and wilted. Remove all the affected plants and destroy them. The good news, however, is that once the soil has rested for a season the aphids will have disappeared.

Whitefly affects maturing brassicas. If the infestation is very bad the leaves will be badly disfigured and the harvest reduced. There are still a few chemical sprays on the market that are effective, but the plants will need to be treated every two weeks for at least a couple of months. The biological control, encarsia formosa, a parasitic wasp, can only be used under glass: they simply fly away outdoors. However, a light infestation is common especially towards the end of the summer and the brassicas are not seriously affected. Soaking them in a bowl of salted water before cooking will kill off any winged stragglers.

Flea beetle attacks mostly seedlings of brassicas including other cruciferous plants such as turnips, swedes and radishes, and can be a serious pest of salad rocket (*see* 'Salads' below). They are minute insects that make thousands of tiny holes in vulnerable young leaves, especially at ground level. If you run your hand over the leaves, flea beetles will jump up in the air. The adults overwinter in fallen leaves and on the remainders of other plants such as wallflowers, nasturtiums and cleome. Then in spring they jump up onto brassica seedlings and can decimate a row in a few days. At present, there are systemic insecticides available for use on seedlings, but it is preferable to ensure that seed germinates fast by sowing into warm soil and then grows away quickly, thereby avoiding the attention of flea beetles.

Greenfly and blackfly can also be a problem. Use either an aphicide that does not affect other insects, or encourage predatory native insects by growing *Tagetes* alongside rows of brassicas (*see* Chapter 10).

Broccoli

Although broccoli takes a long time to produce a crop, it's worth waiting for. It quietly grows through the summer in the background while the showier vegetables are on display and then really comes into its own. Just a few broccoli plants will provide lots of fresh, crisp vegetables at a time when there is little else available to pick for Sunday lunch. Pick the spears as they form, starting with the largest one on top. Once the flowers open the plants will stop producing more spears.

Its relation, calabrese, is somewhat trickier to grow well. Like cauliflower, calabrese often fails to make a dense head and when it does it tends to harbour caterpillars.

Seed facts:

- Seed can be sown in plugs or small pots in the greenhouse in March and planted out before the seedlings become stressed. The roots should be just growing out of the bottom and the leaves should be green, not flushed purple.
- Seed takes between seven to twelve days to germinate.
- Sow the seed outdoors very thinly at a depth of no more than 1cm (0.4in).
- Choose a position that is sheltered from the prevailing wind: the plants have to stand throughout the autumn and winter.
- When the seedlings are planted out they will be bigger and more resistant to the attentions of slugs and snails.
- If you are planting in rows, ensure that they are about 23cm (9in) apart.
- Thin the seedlings when their first true leaves appear, leaving about 60cm (24in) between the plants.
- In an average year, broccoli takes forty weeks to mature, but winter weather conditions can make a big difference.

Maintenance:

- Keep them clear of weeds and netted throughout the year.
- Stake the plants as they become taller; firm them in with the heel of your boot if they become rocky in the wind.
- They will need watering in dry weather and mulching will help conserve that moisture.

Recommended varieties:

- *Early Purple Sprouting Rudolph*
  This variety produces fat, purple spears from September until February.
- *Early White Sprouting White Eye (AGM)*
  Creamy white spears make a change from the purple. This prolific variety crops from late February until April.
- *Late Purple Sprouting (AGM)*
  This broccoli follows on from Rudolph. It's an easy and very hardy variety that fills a 'hungry gap' between late March and April.

Brussels Sprouts

Home-grown and freshly picked small sprouts are a world away from the sulphurous varieties on sale for Christmas lunch. It's definitely worth growing just a few plants. Each plant will produce a succession of sweet little sprouts over a long time and the season can be finished off by picking the top knots of tender leaves and cooking them like cabbage.

There are very attractive purple sprouts that would suit an ornamental garden well. The colour seems to intensify after a few frosts and will be retained if they are steamed or put in the microwave.

Seed facts:

- Most seed is F^1 hybrid so do not save the seed.
- Seed can be sown in plugs or small pots in the greenhouse in early March and seedlings planted out before they become stressed.
- Seed should germinate in seven to twelve days.
- Sow the seed outdoors very thinly at a depth of no more than 1cm (0.4in).
- If you want to make another row it should be 23cm (9in) apart from the first.
- The time between sowing and harvesting depends very much on the variety. It can vary between twenty-eight to thirty-six weeks.

Maintenance:

- When the outdoor-sown seedlings are about 15cm (6in) high, thin them to leave about 75cm (30in) between plants.
- Seedlings that have been raised in containers should be planted so that the lowest pair of their leaves is at soil level. They should be well firmed in with the heel of your boot and watered.
- Keep the plants free of weeds and well watered.
- They respond well to the application of liquid seaweed fertilizer in early summer.
- Stake tall plants before the wind can rock them.

Recommended varieties:

- *Early Half Tall*
  A dwarf variety that produces sweet button sprouts early in the season. This would be very suitable to plant in a small bed.

- *Red Bull*
  Dark purple-red buttons retain their colour and have a mild flavour. Try them stir-fried or steamed.
- *Trafalgar*
  This variety claims to have an especially sweet flavour producing lots of medium-sized sprouts from December until March.

Cabbages

The hearty world of cabbages is a large one. There are varieties to be picked on every day of the year. Some have loose hearts, while others have solid heads ideal for coleslaw. Red cabbages are among the most beautiful plants in the vegetable world and when slow-cooked with apples, onions, honey and wine vinegar they are the ultimate accompaniment to roast pork.

Spring varieties are planted in autumn to provide 'spring greens' the following year. They have conical heads and are generally looser and smaller than summer and winter varieties. Cabbages that mature in midsummer are rounder and tend to have harder heads. Winter cabbages start to mature in autumn and carry on throughout the winter, depending on the variety. These include the crinkly savoy cabbages that are so decorative and hardy.

Seed facts:

- Summer varieties can be sown under glass in February.
- Most cabbage seed will germinate in seven to twelve days.
- Plant them out in early April leaving 45cm (18in) between the plants if they are a compact variety, or 60cm (24in) if the variety is larger.
- Winter varieties should be sown outdoors at the end of April or in May.
- Spring varieties are sown during July and August.
- Sow the seed thinly at a depth of 1cm (0.4in).
- If you want another row it should be 23cm (9in) apart from the first.
- Thin the seedlings of spring varieties in February and March, leaving about 45cm between the plants. The larger thinnings will be big enough to cook.

- Thin the seedlings of winter varieties during June, leaving them the same distance apart as the summer varieties.
- Spring varieties should take about thirty-five weeks to mature.
- Summer and winter varieties take twenty to thirty-five weeks from sowing to harvest.

Maintenance:

- Keep cabbages weeded and watered.
- Firm down any overwintering plants that have been loosened by the frost or high winds.

Recommended varieties:

Spring:

- *Durham Early*
  A medium-sized variety with a good flavour. It can be thinned to produce 'spring greens' before it matures.

- *Pixie (AGM)*
  This is a compact variety on a smaller plant than usual. It has the advantage of only needing to be about 30cm (12in) apart, so could find a place in a smaller bed or container.

Summer:

- *Cape Horn (F¹ hybrid)*
  This has a good flavour and a crisp texture. If it's sown in the greenhouse in February it will produce heads in early June.
- *Hispi (AGM)*
  This is an old favourite with a delicious flavour. It can be spaced more closely than usual as it produces fewer outer leaves and is resistant to bolting. If it's sown in January or February it will produce heads by late spring that will fill the 'hungry gap'.
- *Surprise (F¹ hybrid)*
  This variety produces smoothly rounded pale green heads that would look good next to red

Spring cabbage.

Red cabbage.

cabbages. It's especially sweet taste makes it ideal for making coleslaw for summer salads. And it stands for a long time without the heads splitting.

Winter:

- *Kilaxy*
  This new variety claims to have good resistance to club root disease and is slow to show signs of going black internally. Its shiny round heads are tender, with a good flavour.
- *Robin (F¹ hybrid)*
  A hybrid from the traditional January King that is renowned for its hardiness and ability to stand through the winter. It has a shiny red flush to its heads and the leaves are a deep sea-green.

Red:

- *Red Rookie (AGM) (F¹ hybrid)*
  Solid round red heads that glow out from the vegetable garden in autumn and winter. If this variety is sown under glass in February it will be ready to pick from mid-August onwards.
- *Ruby Perfection (F¹ hybrid)*
  This is a more compact variety that would be especially suitable for a container or for small potager beds.

Savoy:

- *Endeavour (AGM) (F¹ hybrid)*
  This new variety stands throughout the winter in good condition. Its puckered leaves are decorative and it makes firm hearts with a good sweet flavour.

Curly kale 'Redbor'.

Kale

Winter kale has come out of the shadows in recent years and into the forefront of fashionable vegetable society. It has plenty to offer ornamental vegetable gardeners. The scrunchy leaves are very decorative in the garden, especially the darker varieties, and they are extremely winter hardy and tolerant of less than perfect soil too. Their leaves should be picked small and tender for cooking as 'greens'.

Seed facts:

- Sow during April and May directly into soil without disturbing the surface too much.

- Sow the seed very thinly, about 1cm (0.4in) deep.
- The seed should take between seven to twelve days to germinate.
- They can be started off in pots and planted out when they are about 15cm (6in) high.
- The plants should be about 60cm (24in) apart and any rows should be staggered and about 23cm (9in) apart.
- Tread the ground down firmly between the plants.
- Plants should mature between thirty to thirty-six weeks depending on the variety.

Maintenance:

- Keep the plants weed-free and well watered.
- Tread them down firmly to prevent them from rocking in winter.

Recommended varieties:

- *Cavolo de Nero*
  Italian black kale is now very fashionable and is absolutely delicious.
- *Dwarf Green Curled*
  This variety is compact enough to find a place in the smallest plot.
- *Redbor*
  This is one of the most colourful of vegetables, which would win a place in the garden on its beauty alone. It produces tender leaves through-out the winter.

Kohl Rabi

Is it a root, or is it a cabbage? The answer is that it's both a member of the brassica family and the swollen stems look like a root vegetable. These purple or white globes are highly decorative sitting on the surface of the soil in the summer and early autumn. They are easy to grow and have a unique flavour like a mild turnip. They can be cooked like a root vegetable; used in soups and vegetarian casseroles; or grated into coleslaw and salads. The raw white flesh is sweet and crunchy and full of goodness.

Seed facts:

- The seed is best sown outdoors from late February onwards.

- Sow them successively until May.
- Sow the seeds 1cm (0.4in) deep.
- Rows should be about 30cm (12in) apart
- Thin the seedlings to about 20cm (8in) apart.
- Alternatively, transplant the seedlings when they reach the true-leaf stage.
- They should be 20cm (8in) apart.
- Kohl rabi is best picked when still small. If it gets too big, it becomes rather chewy.

Maintenance:

- The plants are easy to grow in soil that was manured the previous autumn.
- Protect the crop from cabbage white butterflies and pigeons.

Kohl rabi 'Purple Delicacy'.

- Keep the plants weeded and watered while they are expanding in summer.
- They should be ready to harvest between June and September.

Recommended varieties:

- *Green Delicacy*
  This early variety has pale jade-green skin with pure white flesh. Harvest the globes when they are the size of tennis balls.
- *Purple Delicacy*
  This variety has wine-purple globes and stems with dark green leaves. This variety is a little later to be harvested.

Perpetual Spinach or Leaf Beet

Although the leaves of these spinach-like vegetables have a similar flavour to summer spinach, they are much coarser and larger. However, their great advantage lies in the fact that this is a biennial crop, unlike summer spinach, which can quickly run to flower in a hot summer. Severe winter frosts do affect the leaves of perpetual spinach, but if you are patient they will start to grow again in early spring. Pick the young leaves; the larger, coarser leaves are best left in place to feed the plant.

Perpetual spinach is far less susceptible to mildew than summer spinach. Bolting is rarely a problem until the following spring.

Seed facts:

- Sow perpetual spinach in April.
- Sow the seeds in drills in the same way as summer spinach.

Maintenance:

- Thin the seedlings to about 8–10cm (3–4in) apart in the rows.
- Start picking alternate plants for the kitchen as soon as they are big enough. They should be about 30cm (12in) apart ultimately.
- Cut the leaves with scissors or secateurs: don't pull them off. It's all too easy to uproot the entire plant with a hard tug.
- Hoe between the rows.
- Keep all spinach well watered: it has a high water content.

- The plants can be protected with a cloche or straw during the winter in very cold districts.

Recommended varieties:

- *Giant Winter*
  This variety has large dark green wrinkled leaves with a good flavour. It is especially hardy and stands for a long time without bolting.
- *Medania (AGM)*
  This is slow to bolt, so can be used for overwintering or for spring sowing.

Spinach – Summer Varieties

Summer spinach is quite a different plant from so-called perpetual spinach or spinach beet. It is relatively easy to grow and could be popped in between rows of winter vegetables. These would provide a little light shade that would serve to protect the spinach from too much sun. The main problem with summer spinach is its tendency to bolt in hot, dry weather.

The uses and virtues of spinach are many and various, and growing your own increases the flavour, vitamins and minerals it contains. Eat the baby leaves raw in salads. For cooking, rinse the leaves under the tap and merely put them into a large saucepan without adding any extra water. They reduce down very quickly: you will need far more for a serving than you might think.

Common pests and diseases:

- Greenfly are the most troublesome pests. Spray with an aphicide as soon as they are spotted, or use an organic alternative (*see* Chapter 10).
- Slugs and snails can be a menace too, especially when the leaves are young.
- Downy mildew is an increasing problem with spinach. If your crops seem to be affected, dig them out immediately and bin the plants. The best prevention is to buy a modern mildew-resistant variety. Alternatively, buy seeds that are coated with the fungicide Thifam Carbendazim, if available.

Seed facts:

- Sow directly outdoors from early April until the end of June in succession.

- Make a drill 2.5cm (1in) deep with the corner of the rake.
- Any rows should be about 30cm (12in) apart.
- Water the drill first before sowing.
- Seed should be sown thinly along the drill.
- Rake back the soil over the drill and firm it down with the back of the rake.
- Germination takes between twelve to twenty-one days.

Maintenance:

- Thin the seedlings to about 8–10cm (3–4in) apart in the rows.
- Start picking alternate plants for the kitchen as soon as they are big enough. They should be about 30cm (12in) apart ultimately.
- Cut the leaves with scissors or secateurs: don't pull them off. It's all too easy to uproot the entire plant with a hard tug.
- Hoe between the rows.
- Keep all spinach well watered: it has a high water content.

Recommended varieties:

- *America*
  A historic variety of spinach that was named by Italian immigrants to the USA, who would carry this seed in their pockets to the New World as it was such a good variety.
- *Campania (F¹ hybrid) (AGM)*
  This vigorous variety is suitable for young salad leaves, or for cooking when the leaves are larger. It's slow to bolt and is mildew-resistant.
- *Mikado*
  This is an oriental spinach with a distinct flavour. It tends to produce lots of side shoots over a long time: perfect for summer stir-fries.
- *Reddy (F¹ hybrid)*
  The pointed green leaves have dark red stems that make this variety as attractive to grow as it is to eat young and sweet in a salad.
- *Spokane (F¹ hybrid)*
  Not only is this variety mildew-resistant and slow to bolt, it can be sown in February in a sheltered spot and every three weeks thereafter to keep a succession of leaves for salads and cooking.

Swiss Chard

This is really a variety of perpetual spinach, or vice versa. It has much wider midribs than the spinach, but the leaves are similar. However, the midribs and veins can be startlingly coloured and highly decorative. They range in colour from shining white through sunshine yellow to ruby red. They are worth growing for their looks alone, but additionally the whole plant is delicious to eat. Strip the leaves off the stalks and put them aside. Slice the stalks and add them to a stir-fry or steam them: they have a delicate flavour like asparagus. Cook the leaves in the same way as spinach, steaming them in just the water they have been rinsed in. They can also be picked small and young to liven up a salad.

The sowing and maintenance are just the same as for perpetual spinach (*see* above). Swiss chard is vulnerable to winter frosts, but, like perpetual spinach, will regrow in spring.

Coloured midribs of the chard 'Bright Lights'.

Recommended varieties:

- *Bright Lights*
  This seed produces a mixture of vivid-coloured plants for salads or cooking.
- *Ruby Chard*
  The selected red stem variety is ideal for maximum visual impact.
- *Silver Chard*
  The white-stemmed forms have been selected out in this variety.

Legumes

The pea family flourishes in soil that is neither heavy and wet, nor too acid. In areas with acid soil it might be worth raking in a little lime. On all soils, dig in plenty of organic matter to a spade's depth in the early winter. If you are growing in rows, you could incorporate it into the bottom of a shallow trench. Replace the soil and sow or transplant over the top. The roots will soon get down to the nutritious layer below and benefit from the moisture.

All legumes have bacteria growing in nodules on their roots. These bacteria 'fix' nitrogen (*see* Chapter 10). So once the crop has been completely harvested, cut the spent stems and leaves to the ground and put them on the compost heap. Then make use of the nitrogen by planting or sowing a row of leaf vegetables that like lots of nitrogen alongside the legume roots.

Rake over the soil in spring to a fine tilth and include some fertilizer at the dose recommended on the packet.

Common pests and diseases of legumes
Mice and birds love peas as much as small children do. Birds are also fond of the emerging seedlings. When you have sown a row cover it with a length of wire mesh on semicircular hoops like cloches to discourage their attentions.

Once the lines of peas and beans are up and growing away, they are vulnerable to rabbits and occasionally pigeons, which have a fondness for the flowers. In a country garden an enclosing fence will ward off the rabbits (*see* Chapter 10). If pigeons are a nuisance, get out the scarecrow.

Pea moth can be a problem if peas and beans are left a long time on the plant before harvesting.

The moths drill holes into the pods and peas or beans, then their eggs hatch into nasty pale yellow maggots that eat their way out. If they prove to be a problem, sow early maturing varieties for picking by mid-July, or late varieties that can be sown after mid-June when the pea moths have finished laying their eggs. Spraying with an effective chemical would of necessity affect the developing peas.

Powdery mildew can affect peas and beans, especially late crops that are grown into the autumn. It manifests itself as a white powdery down on the leaves, stems and pods. A systemic fungicide is effective, but spraying might be too close to harvesting. If this is a regular problem, it might be better only to grow early crops of legumes that are not so badly affected.

Borlotto Beans
These traditional Italian beans have beautiful red and white streaked pods that would look very decorative on a wigwam or climbing up any contrivance in the ornamental vegetable garden.

They are not eaten as fresh beans, but left on the vine until they start to dry out. They can then be picked, shelled and either eaten straightaway or frozen. There will be no need to soak them overnight like haricot beans, as they will cook in forty minutes from frozen or half an hour when they are fresh. The beans themselves are red and white and are delicious in casseroles, soups and underneath slow-roasted lamb with rosemary.

Seed facts:

- Discard any seeds that are shrivelled or damaged.
- Sow the beans two to a pot in a frost-free greenhouse in April, thinning out the weaker specimen and planting them out when they have hardened off in May.
- Position one plant either side of the stakes of a wigwam, about 30cm (12in) apart ideally.
- Protect the young plants from both slug and snail damage.

Maintenance:

- Tie in the shoots as they extend upwards.
- Keep the plants weed-free, and watered in dry spells.

- It helps to mulch the plants to conserve the moisture.
- Spraying the open flowers with water in dry weather will help them to set.

Recommended varieties:

- *Centofiamme (100 Flames)*
- *Lingua di Fuoco (Firetongue)*
  These are both traditional Italian climbing varieties.
- *Solista*
  This is another climbing variety but with more beans per pod (about eight to nine). It has good disease resistance.

- *Supremo*
  This dwarf bush-forming variety would be suitable for smaller beds. It has good disease resistance also.

Broad Beans
Broad beans may not at first sight appear to be the most ornamental of vegetables, but they mature at a time when there is little else in the garden. Among the most useful are the Longpod varieties that are traditionally sown before Christmas and crop in late May to June.

These early plants are less plagued by blackfly, which can infest the later plants. Usually Longpod varieties have already produced their beans by the time the blackfly are up and about in spring and

A row of broad beans in June.

they also tend to have tougher shoots that are a bit too chewy for blackfly teeth. Plant a few French Marigolds nearby to harbour hoverfly larvae that love to feast on blackfly (*see* Chapter 10).

Anyone who has had to endure huge broad beans in leather coats may have been put off for life. But if you grow your own you have the chance to pick them small, sweet and meltingly tender. You may even find your family demanding more. Once they are converted to broad beans you could try some of the spring-sown varieties. The trick is simply to pick them small. You could always leave the remainder for seed or the compost heap.

Seed facts:

- Discard any seed that has small round holes.
- Longpod varieties should be sown in November.
- Other varieties can be sown from the end of February until early May in succession.
- They should germinate in ten to fourteen days.
- If you sow in the spring they will take about sixteen weeks to be ready for picking.
- The Longpod varieties take between eighteen to twenty-eight weeks from sowing, although in a severe winter some of the Longpod seedlings will be lost.
- Sow the Longpod varieties in soil that was improved with organic matter for a previous crop. Too much fertilizer in winter will produce soft, vulnerable growth.
- Sow the seed about 5cm (2in) deep, in shallow drills about 20cm (8in) apart.
- A second drill should be 20cm (8in) from the first.
- Another double row would need to be 60cm (24in) from the first pair.
- Rake the soil back over the rows, invert the rake and tamp it down lightly along the rows. Mark each row with the seed name and date sown.

Maintenance:

- Keep the plants weed-free, and watered in dry spells.
- As the plants grow they become top-heavy so they will need stakes to prevent them toppling in the wind.

French marigolds help to keep the broad beans clear of blackfly.

- Pinch off the tip of the shoots as soon as the flowers set beans. This will speed up the harvest and helps to prevent blackfly attack.

Recommended varieties:

- *Aquadulce Claudia (AGM)*
  This is the classic variety to sow in November for overwintering.
  It will grow to about 90–100cm (36–40in), so will need staking in spring.
- *Stereo*
  This is a new spring-sown variety with slender pods that can be eaten whole, like mangetout peas. It grows to 90cm (35in), so will need

staking. If it is picked regularly it will keep producing more.

- *The Sutton (AGM)*
  A spring-sown variety, it only grows to 30cm (12in), making it ideal for the small beds of an ornamental vegetable garden. The beans are especially sweet and tender.

French Beans

French beans are delicious hot or in salads, especially if they are picked young and slim. The coloured varieties are very decorative, and they will even produce plenty of beans in a container on a sunny terrace.

The conventional dwarf or bush French beans are either round-podded like a pencil, or have flat pods. The former are completely stringless, but many of the flat-podded varieties can become rather stringy once they are past their youth.

Seed facts:

- The seed will rot if it's planted too early. Sow two to a pot in a frost-free greenhouse in April, thinning out the weaker specimen.
- Seeds take fourteen to twenty days to germinate.
- Plant them out when they have hardened off in May.
- Alternatively, sow outdoors in a sheltered sunny site from May until early July in succession.
- Sow the seed about 5cm (2in) deep, in shallow drills about 20cm (8in) apart.
- A second drill should be about 60cm (24in) from the first.
- Plant or sow them in succession, every three to four weeks.
- Plants take approximately ten to thirteen weeks to produce a crop.

Maintenance:

- Protect the seedlings from slugs and snails and keep the rows weeded and watered.
- The bush beans may need the support of some twiggy branches to keep them off the ground.
- Climbing varieties will need a wigwam or something similar.
- If the weather is dry when the flowers are out, a light spray of water will help them to set.

Recommended varieties:

- *Blauhilde*
  A climbing French bean that produces bunches of stringless purple pods which are slightly flattened. They would look good growing amongst sweet peas.
- *Cobra (AGM)*
  Tender green pencil pods. This variety has violet flowers that would earn a place in any ornamental vegetable garden.
- *Golden Teepee*
  Creamy yellow pencil pods are held above the foliage. They have a good flavour and are stringless.
- *Goldfield*
  This climbing French bean produces its bright yellow flat wax-pods over a long period.

Climbing French bean 'Purple Teepee'.

- *Maxi*
  Bush-forming beans that are held well above the foliage out of reach of slimy molluscs and within easy view of the harvester. The pencil beans are high-yielding and very tender.
- *Purple Teepee*
  Another dwarf bush with attractive purple pencil pods held high above the leaves. They turn dark green in boiling water.

Peas, Sugar Snaps and Mangetout

Although peas can be quite difficult to grow successfully, there is nothing to beat the flavour of freshly picked and shelled petits pois. They should be cooked immediately for the sweetest taste. Even after just half an hour's storage, the peas' sugars turn to starch.

Mangetout peas crop for far longer than conventional peas: their motherhood is constantly thwarted because their shells are picked before the peas or seeds have had a chance to develop. So the plant keeps trying. Sugar snap peas are much fleshier than Mangetout and they too crop for much longer.

Asparagus peas are a little different: they have winged pods and very attractive red flowers. As their name suggests, they have the distinctive and delicious flavour of asparagus rather than peas.

Most peas need support of some kind. A wigwam of hazel twigs is very effective in a small plot, or train them along a row of 1m (39in) high twigs. Insert the supports as soon as the seedlings are safe from mice and birds.

Peas divide themselves into two distinct types: the round-seeded varieties that are the hardiest; and the wrinkled varieties that are larger and sweeter. Round varieties can be sown in the autumn under cloches to produce a crop in May and June. Then there are first early, second early and maincrop varieties, just like potatoes. These could provide a further succession of crops if they are planted at the right times.

Common pests and diseases:

- Mice can't wait to dig up the seeds the moment you have sown them. Protect the rows with lengths of fine-mesh wire netting, about 30cm (12in) wide. Bend them into a half-tunnel and stake them down over the row. Use a bit of spare netting for each end.
- Pea moth can become a severe problem if crop rotation (*see* Chapter 7) is not followed in your garden. The adults emerge from cocoons that overwinter in the soil, between the end of May to early August, just as the peas are flowering. They lay eggs on the pods and the emerging caterpillars bore into them. They are only apparent when the peas are shelled for cooking. Plant the peas early or late to avoid the moths, or cover them with horticultural fleece, which is effective though not very ornamental. A pea moth pheromone trap hung between the plants will deceive their amorous intentions. If the infestation is severe and frequent, then don't grow sweet peas for a year or two and ensure that there is no vetch growing nearby.

Seed facts:

- Peas need a site that is away from fences and walls: they need lots of moisture in the soil.
- They are, however, more tolerant of a little shade than most legumes.
- Apply a dose of organic fertilizer to the soil prior to sowing.
- Sow a suitable round variety in October to November to crop in May to June.
- First early varieties are sown in March to April to crop in June to July.
- Second early wrinkled varieties are sown in April to May to produce an August crop.
- A suitable wrinkled variety can also be sown in June to July to crop in September.
- Make a shallow trench about 7cm (2¾in) deep and about 15cm (6in) wide.
- Rows should be about the width of the expected height of the crop apart.
- Scatter pea seeds thinly along the trench.
- Water the seeds in the bottom of the trench: moisture helps their germination.
- Replace the soil and firm it down lightly.
- Put a wire-mesh tunnel in place to protect the seed from mice.

Maintenance:

- Put in the supporting hazel twigs as soon as the mesh tunnels are removed.
- Keep the plants well watered. Peas should take priority during water shortages.
- Moisture can be conserved in the soil with a mulch of garden compost applied when the soil is wet.
- Hoe regularly to prevent weeds growing and competing between the rows; hand-weed between the plants if possible.
- Pick the peas as soon as they have formed petits pois for the best flavour. Once they get old they become floury and tasteless. However, pick any peas you may have missed earlier anyway: the more that are left, the fewer the plant will produce. It will have achieved motherhood.
- Use two hands to pick peas: it's easy to tear away the entire stem from the plant.

Recommended varieties:

Peas: autumn:
- *Douce Provence (round)*
  This autumn-sown variety is low growing: about 45cm (18in). It has a good sweet flavour.
- *Meteor (round)*
  From an autumn sowing, this old variety produces lots of small well-filled pods with a good flavour from May. It is more dwarf than Douce Provence at about 35cm (14in).

First early:
- *Misty (AGM)*
  A new variety, Misty produces pairs of short pods bursting with well-flavoured peas. It crops over a long period of time. Height: 60cm (24in).
- *Twinkle*
  This variety crops very quickly from seed, making it an ideal variety for successional planting. It's a dwarf variety that needs no staking. Height: 60cm (24in).

Second early:
- *Greensage*
  This variety has an exceptionally sweet taste. It has long pods with up to ten or eleven peas.

The seed can be sown every ten to fourteen days for successional planting. Height: 75cm (30in).

Maincrop:
- *Alderman (AGM)*
  This is a tall variety suitable for a wigwam that crops well in all parts of the UK. It produces long, full pods and the peas have an excellent flavour. Height: 150cm (59in).
- *Hurst Greenshaft (AGM)*
  Pairs of long pods regularly produce lots of peas with an especially good flavour. This variety is disease-resistant. Height: 75cm (30in).
- *Markana*
  Curiously decorative, this variety has lots of curling tendrils and few leaves, so it may not need staking at all. The peas have a good flavour too. Height: 60cm (24in).

Asparagus pea:
- This is a little known pea that you rarely find in the supermarkets. It's also very decorative with

The red flowers of the Asparagus Pea.

its brick-red flowers and winged seedpods. It needs no staking, but the foliage quite often hides the pods. Height: 30–45cm (12–18in).

- Sow in May, about 2.5cm (1in) deep in ground that has been manured during the winter. Any rows should be about 35cm (14in) apart.
- Pick the pods as small as possible. Top and tail, then steam until they are '*al dente*'.

Mangetout:

- *Carouby de Maussane*
  This French variety is tall and bears attractive purple flowers. Its large pods have a good sweet flavour. Height: 150cm (60in).
- *Dwarf Sugar (AGM)*
  This is the true French Mangetout variety, with an excellent flavour. It will need a little support. Height: 60cm (24in).
- *Golden Sweet*
  The pale green pods and pink flowers are particularly attractive in a potager. The pods are sweet and delicious too. It's tall enough to grow well over a wigwam. Height: 180cm (71in).

Sugar snap:

- *Cascadia (AGM)*
  These rounded pods are sweet and crisp for salads or steaming, remaining tender for longer than most varieties. It has good disease resistance too. Height: 90cm (35in).
- *Sugar Ann (AGM)*
  Bred for flavour, this variety is also high yielding. Pods can be left on the plant and will produce mature peas later. Height: 75–90cm (30–35in).

Runner Beans

These are among the most rewarding and decorative of vegetables. Runners keep on cropping from mid-summer until the autumn, providing mountains of crisp, sweet beans. There are varieties with all-white, all-pink, or red and white flowers if you want a change from the scarlet.

Pick them young before they have developed leathery skins and indigestible strings. Any that have got too big should also be picked to prevent the plant from achieving motherhood. If you don't want to eat them, they can be composted. But if you want to save seed for next year, leave a few biggies at the end of the season to mature on the plant. Pick them and dry them off in a frost-free shed or garage, then shell them and keep them in a paper bag, in a sealed plastic box in the fridge.

Seed facts:

- Runner beans will not succeed in very cold areas.
- They take about ten to fourteen days to germinate in the greenhouse, so sow them in April at the earliest or they will become too big for their boots before they can be planted out.
- They can be sown outdoors in May after the danger of frost has passed.

Runner beans just right for picking: small, sweet and stringless.

A traditional all-red flowered variety.

- If you sow them outdoors you should protect them from mice.
- They should take twelve to fourteen weeks from sowing to harvesting.
- Runner beans are climbers, so their supports need protection from wind.
- At least a month before sowing or planting outdoors dig in organic matter about 45cm (18in) deep.
- Construct a wigwam or a row of traditional supports.

Maintenance:

- Tie in the first climbing shoots to the supports to show them the way.
- Protect the young plants from slugs and snails.
- Mulching the young plants will help to conserve moisture.
- When the shoots reach the top of their supports, snip them out to keep the beans within comfortable reach for harvesting.

- Spray the flowers with water during dry, sunny spells to help them to set.
- Plants benefit from a high potash liquid feed during July and August.
- Pick the beans regularly or the plant will stop producing them.

Recommended varieties:

- *Hestia*
  This is a dwarf bush variety with pretty red and white flowers which produces slim, stringless beans quite early in the season. It's ideal for a large container.
- *Painted Lady*
  An old red and white flowered variety that produces lots of tender beans with a good, old-fashioned flavour.
- *White Lady (AGM)*
  The white flowers are more attractive to us than to the birds. They ignore them for longer. This variety is also said to cope better with higher summer temperatures.

Root vegetables

Prepare the soil before sowing any root vegetable by weeding and raking it over to produce a fine, crumbly texture: a 'tilth'. Take care to remove any stones, but do not add any organic matter either during the previous winter or in spring. These factors cause the tap roots to 'fork'. However, the soil should be in good heart from the previous crop of either legumes or brassicas. Ideally, root vegetables should follow brassicas as the whole area will have been manured the year before, rather than after peas and beans that were grown in a random pattern of trenches and holes. These would have been filled the previous year with organic matter, which might tempt the roots into forking.

Most root vegetables are sown directly into the soil: transplanting anything with a tap root is not a practical option. It's important to thin the seedlings quickly to give each selected plant the best start from the nutrients and moisture available. Tap roots also have a tendency to intertwine if they are left to develop too closely for too long.

Rows of root vegetables in early summer.

Common pests and diseases of root vegetables

Carrot fly is perhaps the most damaging of all root vegetable pests. Most of the chemical solutions are no longer on the market, but there are new carrot varieties that have been bred to be resistant to their attentions (*see* below). There are also lots of organic methods that are very effective (*see* Chapter 10).

Carrots often split when it rains following a prolonged dry spell: the sudden moisture swells the roots too quickly.

Scab not only affects potatoes, but beetroots and radishes may also display symptoms of this condition. It's not one disease, but a general term that describes the damage usually caused by fungal diseases of the skin of the roots. The skin is blemished by a shallow scab that is mostly only disfiguring: it rarely damages the crop. Scab usually occurs in very limey soils, so make sure you dig in plenty of organic matter for the previous crop.

If root vegetables are left in the soil during the autumn and early winter, any physical damage to the skin provides an inlet for soil-living slugs. So lift the crop in the early autumn and use or freeze it straightaway. Mature roots can also be stored in dry commercial compost or peat in a dark, cool, frost-free shed – but watch out for marauding mice.

Beetroot

Not only are beetroot one of the new 'superfoods', but their sweet flavour is appreciated by all the family. Their dark green leaves with ruby-red veins and stems make them one of the most decorative vegetables too. And these pretty young leaves are also delicious in salads.

There are varieties with white, striped and yellow flesh, as well as the usual red. Pick them while they are still small: once they get bigger than a tennis ball they become fibrous and unpleasant to eat. Don't peel the roots before you boil them, just wash off any soil and twist off the leaves, allowing about 5cm (2in) of stalks to remain, otherwise they will 'bleed' and lose their lovely colour when cooked.

Seed facts:

- The 'seeds' are really clusters of individuals, so thinning out is mostly unavoidable.
- It helps to speed up germination if the seed is soaked overnight.
- Rake in a seaweed fertilizer before sowing.
- Sow in late April to May. The variety Pronto can be sown as late as the end of July.
- The seed will take between twelve to twenty-one days to germinate.
- Sow the seed clusters at a depth of about 2.5cm (1in) about 10cm (4in) apart in the row.
- Rows should be about 30cm (12in) apart.
- It takes about nine weeks from sowing to picking the first roots. Larger roots will take about sixteen weeks to mature.

Maintenance:

- Thin out the seedlings, leaving just the single strongest one in each position.

Red-stemmed beetroot.

- Take care when you hoe not to nick the seedlings.
- Keep the plants well watered, or the roots will become fibrous.
- Mulch the seedlings when they are a reasonable size to retain the moisture.

Recommended varieties:

- *Albina Vereduna*
  This variety has pure white bulbs with a very sweet flesh. Its green leaves are curled and wavy and excellent for salads. It would make an ideal neighbour to a traditional red variety.

- *Bull's Blood*
  This is a highly decorative variety grown for its dark red leaves. They are attractive in any position in the garden or container. Their leaves are delicious added to a baby-leaf salad.

- *Chiogga Pink*
  This variety has dark green leaves and ruby-red stems. The roots have orange-pink skin and a bull's-eye of sweet red and white flesh within. It fades to pink when cooked.

- *Golden Beet*
  To ring the changes in the garden and on the plate, this variety has vivid orange-yellow flesh

that does not bleed so easily when cooked. It tastes good too.

- *Pronto*
  This is a variety that is grown for its small-sized roots. It's excellent for successional sowing as it will crop from sowings made as late as early July.

Carrots

Carrots would win their way into every vegetable garden, decorative or not, on their flavour alone. A home-grown, freshly picked bunch of carrots is sweet enough to eat raw and grated; sliced and steamed; or, if especially young and small, blanched and served with a knob of butter. There are many varieties to choose from: purple-skinned, ball-shaped, or those with pale honey-coloured flesh.

Common pests and diseases:

- The main problem with growing carrots is the carrot root fly. This bores its way into the shoulders of the root as it grows laying its eggs that hatch into wriggly little maggots. The adult flies are attracted to carrots by their smell, which is particularly strong when the roots are being thinned. There are quite a few different ways to defeat this pest (*see* Chapter 10), but one of the surest is to grow those varieties that are partially resistant. These have been bred with lower levels of chlorogenic acid in the developing roots. If you have the space you could sow another non-resistant variety that will attract the fly away from the partially resistant types.

Seed facts:

- Seed has to be sown directly into the soil because of the shape of the roots.
- It can be sown as soon as the soil warms in spring: usually during March.
- Make a drill with the corner of the rake about 1–1.5cm (0.4–0.6in) deep and sow very thinly.
- It is essential to sow thinly to minimize disturbance of the remaining roots when they are thinned.
- Seed takes about fourteen days to germinate.
- Most carrots take between fourteen and sixteen weeks to make a full-sized root, but you can pull them sooner if you prefer them smaller.

- Carrots can be sown in succession. Later sowings in June may avoid the attentions of the carrot root fly (*see* above).
- Short-rooted varieties can be sown in August long after the root fly has flown. They should be covered with bell jars or cloches in October, then pulled in November.

Maintenance:

- Thinning will have to take place or the roots will intertwine. Later thinnings are suitable for cooking.
- Keep the crop weed-free and well watered in dry spells. A downpour of rain following a drought can cause the roots to split.

Recommended varieties:

- *Crème de Lite (F¹ hybrid)*
  Although this is not a resistant variety, it has sweet, tapered roots with a cream-coloured flesh (*see* Chapter 10 for tips on avoiding the attentions of the carrot root fly).
- *Flyaway (F¹ hybrid)*
  Sweet, blunt-nosed carrots that are partially resistant to carrot root fly. This is an early summer variety that continues into the autumn.
- *Parisien Market*
  This small, round French variety would be suitable for containers. Carrot root fly has a low flight path, so by growing plants at a height in a container you avoid their attentions.
- *Purple Haze*
  This purple-skinned variety has a bright orange heart. It makes an interesting and sweet-tasting addition to salads.
- *Resistafly (F¹ hybrid)*
  This is another fly-resistant variety that crops later in the summer and can be stored for the winter. It has larger roots, and it has a good sweet flavour.

Parsnips

Although not especially ornamental in growth, parsnips are such a stalwart winter vegetable that growing just a few in a corner of the plot is well worth the space they occupy.

Carrots and parsnips in summer.

Their sweet flavour is enhanced by roasting until they caramelize, plus they make one of the most deliciously warming winter soups. Parsnips are better and sweeter after a few frosts, as these turn the carbohydrates and starches in the root into sugars and topple the foliage. You will need to mark the row clearly so that you don't spike their crowns with a fork when you lift them.

The shorter-rooted varieties are easier to grow: it can be difficult to extract the tip from a deeply fertile soil if it is a long-rooted variety. The roots can be left in the soil throughout the winter, although the cores do become rather too woody to eat by early spring.

Common pests and diseases:

- Parsnips are generally fairly trouble-free, although parsnip canker can be a nuisance. It is a fungal disease that enters the root through any mechanical damage caused by careless hoeing, or occasionally by the attentions of the carrot root fly. Rusty-coloured patches develop, usually as the roots reach maturity, and they can spread down through the entire system. So, ideally, parsnips should be grown as far away from carrots as possible if canker is a recurrent problem. Cover the shoulders of the roots with soil as they develop, taking care not to damage them when hoeing. Canker is more frequent in acid soils, so put down a little lime before sowing if necessary. Any affected parsnips should be dug up and removed to prevent the spread of the fungus, and make sure they are grown in a different area the following year.

Seed facts:

- Choose a draining site.
- Rake the soil to a fine tilth.
- Sow the seeds as soon as the ground starts to warm up in spring: from the end of February until April.
- The seed is thin and papery, so choose a still day to sow.
- Sow the seed thinly in a drill made with the corner of the rake about 1cm (0.4in) deep.
- Draw the soil back over the drill and firm down the soil with the back of the rake.
- Rows should be about 30cm (12in) apart.

Maintenance:

- Thin the seedlings to leave one plant at about 15–20cm (6–8in) intervals.
- Because parsnips have a tapering tap root they cannot be transplanted.
- Keep the weeds down by hoeing carefully between the plants and rows.
- They will be ready to lift after the first ground frost when the foliage will have dropped.
- In colder areas of the country they can be lifted before any extreme weather and stored in a black plastic bag in a frost-free shed or garage. However, their quality will be impaired; it's better to leave them in the ground if possible.

Recommended varieties:

- *Avonresister*
  This old favourite has small, conical roots that are especially suitable for shallower soils and raised beds. It has a good flavour too.
- *Countess (F¹ hybrid)*
  This is a new variety that has been bred for its smooth white roots that retain their colour well after washing. It has conical roots with shallow crowns and can be stored well into the spring.
- *Gladiator (F¹ hybrid)*
  Bred for its resistance to canker and with plenty of vigour, this variety is easy to grow and has a clean white skin.
- *Tender and True (AGM)*
  This traditional variety has been popular for a long time. It has an especially good flavour and is resistant to canker.

Salsify

The 'vegetable oyster' is far more popular in the rest of Europe than it is in the UK. Its long thin roots, rather like a skinny parsnip, have a sweetly delicate flavour reminiscent of asparagus. They are well worth the extra trouble of cleaning them. Stand the prepared salsify in water containing a drop or two of vinegar to prevent the creamy flesh from discolouring, then steam them gently.

Seed facts:

- Sow three seeds at 15cm (6in) intervals along the row in April.
- Thin the seedlings to leave the strongest as soon as possible to prevent them intertwining.
- Keep the plants well weeded and watered.
- The roots should be ready from autumn onwards and can remain in the soil all winter.
- If you leave them in the ground to flower the following year, they are a very ornamental addition to the potager.

Alliums – the onion family

The onion family (*Allium*) comprises a wide range of different forms, ranging from chives, pickling and

Salsify flowers.

spring onions to large maincrop onions for storing in winter and Japanese varieties that mature earlier than the traditional types.

All members of the onion family like to grow in a sunny spot in ground that has been prepared with plenty of organic matter during the previous winter. They are greedy vegetables and take up space during the peak time of the growing year. But there are some varieties that are well worth accommodating.

Growing maincrop onions from seed is usually only undertaken by growers of giant vegetables. It's far easier to grow them from sets, that is, small onions that have already been growing from seed for a season. Onions are biennials. They produce their leaves and bulbs in their first season and then flower in the second year. Consequently, if you are growing them from sets you have to deceive them

Chive flowers.

into thinking that they are still in their first season, otherwise they will run to flower, or 'bolt'. So it's essential that untreated sets are stored somewhere frost-free: a garage or well-insulated garden shed. Buy them during the early winter so that you can ensure they are stored correctly. And don't be in too much of a hurry in spring to plant them out: a few nights of late spring frost will cause them to bolt. Spread the sets out in a light place to prevent them sprouting too early and keep them cool. Alternatively, most seed companies sell specially prepared onion sets that have been heat-treated for twenty weeks. The heat treatment destroys the embryonic flower bud at the centre of the onion set. So even after a long cold spring these prepared onions will not run to flower.

Shallots seem less prone to bolting, but it makes sense not to plant them too early in spring either. Certain varieties of garlic are suitable for planting in autumn without any danger of bolting.

Common pests and diseases of the Allium *family*

White rot is the most serious infection of all members of the onion family. It affects leeks, chives and all forms of onions, including ornamental *Alliums* in the flower garden. They wilt at first and then collapse above ground, while the bulbs become infected with a fluffy white fungus and then rot. The infected plants must be lifted and destroyed and the soil they were growing in should be dug out and disposed of. The fungus is at present untreatable and its spores remain in the soil for up to fifteen years. Any member of the *Allium* family will be infected if it is grown in the same soil. If white rot is present, you will need to grow all the onions in a completely separate part of the vegetable garden in future. There is no chemical control, but maintaining a four-year rotation in future will help with prevention.

Onion neck rot affects immature bulbs either in the ground, or if they are stored before they have been fully ripened. The neck of the onion becomes pale brown and mushy and gradually the rot spreads throughout the bulb and its neighbours. It can be avoided with a fertilizer high in potash during the growing season. And take care not to nick the onions when you are hoeing the bed.

Onion fly lays its eggs in spring on the leaves and in the soil at the base of the onion or leek. These hatch into little white maggots that tunnel into the bulb or stem. Young plants wilt and die, while larger, more mature plants turn soft and rot at the base. The moment this problem is spotted the onions or leeks should be dug out thoroughly and destroyed, otherwise the maggots pupate in the soil ready to hatch out and repeat the process next year. After harvesting even healthy leeks and onions, be sure to gather up all the debris left on the soil.

Rust manifests itself as raised orange spots on the leaves. One rust infects garlic, onions and chives, while a related form affects leeks. Onion rust cannot spread to leeks, or vice versa. It is not usually serious enough to kill the plants that are damaged.

It tends to affect leeks or onions that are grown too close together, especially if the soil has been well manured. A dressing of potash, or liquid tomato fertilizer would help its prevention if it has been a problem in the past. Don't put infected leaves on the compost heap or the spores will live to fight another day. There are resistant varieties of leeks that have been bred in recent years (*see* below).

Garlic

Perhaps the most pungent of the onion family, garlic needs no introduction. It enhances flavour and is famously good for your health. It's believed to have been eaten since the nomads crossed Europe after the last Ice Age.

Garlic tends to divide itself into two groups: the softneck type, which is easy to grow, has smaller cloves and stores well. The hardneck garlic, with thinner skins and larger cloves, stores less well. And there are very many other forms of garlic available on-line that suit various different styles of cuisine, from Creole to Chinese.

The 'scapes', also known as 'rocamboles', that is, the emerging flower stalks, are good to eat either in salads or stir-fries. Or chop them up, fry them in a little olive oil and mash them into potato. The flowers, if they are produced, are delicious too.

Store the garlic bulbs in a frost-free shed, not a warm garage, or they will start to sprout too early and these early-sprouting corms will not form bulbs.

Set facts:

- The site should be sunny and free-draining.
- Plenty of organic matter should have been incorporated into the soil before planting.
- Garlic should be planted between mid-September and early November for the best crop yield.
- Garlic needs a cold spell of at least a month to make bulbs.
- In colder parts of the country it can be planted in early spring, but this usually results in a smaller crop. Plant the individual cloves 10cm (4in) apart.
- The rows should be about 30cm (12in) apart.
- Push them down firmly so that only the tip projects above the soil, then heel them in lightly.

Maintenance:

- In mild areas the bulbs will not need any protection over the winter.
- In colder parts, or during an especially cold winter, cover the cloves with horticultural fleece.
- Apply a high-nitrogen feed once or twice in April and May.
- Keep the bulbs well watered in dry spells from spring onwards.
- Once the bulb has formed and finished growing, allow it to dry out. Too much water at this stage will cause the bulb to rot.
- Be sure to keep on top of the weeding: garlic is shallow-rooted.

Recommended varieties:

- *Elephant*
  Actually not a true garlic, but a leek, these huge cloves are very mild; they are delicious roasted with chicken. They are spectacular in the vegetable garden too.
- *Lautrec Wight (hardneck)*
  Despite its name, this variety originates in south-west France. It has deep pink cloves and white skins. Its flavour is exceptionally smooth and creamy.
- *Moldovan (hardneck)*
  An ancient form of garlic with large succulent cloves and rocamboles, its purple-tinged bulbs would also make an attractive addition to the potager.
- *Solent Wight (softneck)*
  This is one of the best varieties bred at the Garlic Farm on the Isle of Wight. It produces large bulbs with a particularly good deep flavour. The bulbs also store well if they are kept cool and dry.

Leeks

Leeks are among the most useful of garden vegetables. They really come into their own in winter when they can remain standing in the soil without any harm until they start to bolt in the spring: that is, if there are any left.

Leeks do not grow well in wet, compacted soil. They do not need quite as rich a soil as onions, but

Neat rows of leeks.

they will grow better in soil that was manured during the previous autumn and winter. They take up very little room, so represent a good return on the space they occupy, plus straight lines of stout white stems look good in the ornamental vegetable garden. Leeks respond well to a dressing of organic fertilizer worked into the soil before transplanting.

The uses of leeks are many and various. The spare thinnings are a perfect substitute for spring onions, either in a salad or in stir-fries. During the winter, leeks are best picked young and slim; as they age, they get tougher and more fibrous.

Alternatively, 'baby' varieties can be sown at monthly intervals from the middle of March until June. These are thinned to about 2.5cm (1in) apart and not transplanted. Pick them as soon as they reach about 1cm (0.4in) thickness.

Seed facts:

- Leeks should be sown in March as soon as the soil has warmed up.
- Sow rows of leeks thinly in a nursery bed in a shallow drill about 1cm (0.4in) deep.
- Rows should be about 23cm (9in) apart.
- Cover the seed drill lightly with a rake and then firm the surface down with the flat of the rake.
- The seeds should germinate in about twenty-one days.
- They will take between thirty-six and forty-five weeks to mature.

Maintenance:

- The young leeks will be ready for transplanting when they are about 20cm (8in) tall and the thickness of a pencil.
- Lift them during a wet spell when the soil is workable, usually in May or June.
- Using a sharp knife or secateurs, trim off the base of the roots to the width of your hand.
- Similarly, cut off the tips of the leaves to the width of your hand.
- If the weather has been consistently dry, give the seedlings and the new bed a good watering the evening before.
- Prepare the new bed by raking in some organic fertilizer at the recommended rate.
- Rows of transplanted leeks should be about 30cm (12in) apart, leaving a gap of about 15cm (6in) between the individual plants.
- Using a dibber (*see* 'Useful and Essential Garden Tools', Chapter 3), make holes about 15cm (6in) deep and drop in the fattest of the young leeks.
- Do not backfill the hole with soil.
- Continue down the rows until all the plants have been inserted, then water them with a fine rose on the watering can.
- The water will settle the roots in contact with the soil at the bottom. Any subsequent rain will gradually fill in the planting holes.
- Keep the rows weed-free and well watered during dry spells in the summer.
- The length of the white stem can be increased once the leeks are well developed by drawing soil up around the stems in dry weather. Wet soil, however, can cause the stems to rot.

Recommended varieties:

*   *Apollo (AGM)*
    This is an ideal variety for close planting in a small ornamental bed. It produces vigorous stems with a tolerance to fungal rusts.
*   *Blue Solaise*
    This traditional French variety has an exceptionally good flavour. Its deep blue-purple leaves are a positive contribution to the potager.
*   *Edison*
    Treat as a 'baby' variety: there is no need to transplant them. They will, however, stand well until February and their good flavour will remain.
*   *Oarsman (F^1 seed) (AGM)*
    This early variety has exceptionally long stems and no 'bulbing' at the base. They stand well throughout the winter and are resistant to fungal rusts and bolting.
*   *Pandora*
    This variety has a good tolerance of leek rust and is quick to reach maturity: about ninety days after transplanting.

Onions

It would probably take up quite a lot of space to grow enough onions to feed the average family for a season, but there are some that are both decorative and worth finding room for. There is something very ordered about neat rows of onions bubbling on the surface of the soil. Red onions are very decorative both to grow and to slice up and eat. They are sweet and mild enough to add raw to salads and every modern cook makes their own sweet red onion marmalade.

The flavour of all types of onion – the sweetness and mildness – is affected by the soil, the weather and the fundamental sulphur content of the variety. The sweetest flavour is produced on light sandy soils. Heavy clay soils seem to grow stronger, more sulphuric flavours.

A rope of harvested onions hanging in a frost-free dry shed or garage is an easy way of storing them in a small space. Or an old net bag that held bulbs is an adequate, if less attractive, method.

Set facts:

*   When the sets arrive, unpack them and then spread them out in a light, cool but frost-free shed or garage.
*   Trim off the dried tips of the bulbs. If they are planted untrimmed, they will be pulled out of the ground by hooligan birds before they have had a chance to root.
*   They grow best in soil that has been manured in early winter.
*   They appreciate a dressing of organic fertilizer raked into the surface just before planting.
*   Plant heat-treated sets in February and March. Non-treated sets should be kept frost-free before planting in April.
*   Push the sets gently into the prepared beds about 15cm (6in) apart, so that the tips are just showing.
*   Any rows should be about 30cm (12in) apart.
*   They should start to sprout in eleven to fourteen days.
*   Sets take about eighteen weeks to mature.

Maintenance:

*   Push the sets back in if they are disturbed by birds or the weather.
*   Hoe between the onions, taking care not to nick the skins.
*   Firm the soil after hoeing.
*   Give the onions a liquid feed if you want large bulbs.
*   If a flower stem does appear, lift the bulb and use it straightaway.
*   Once the whole crop has finished growing and all the leaves have fallen over, put a fork underneath the bulbs and lift them out of the soil.
*   The bulbs can either dry out on the surface of the soil, or in wet weather lay them out in a greenhouse or beneath a cold frame to dry for a week or two.
*   Any onions that are a bit soft or have thick stems containing a flower stalk should be used straightaway.
*   Once the stems have died and become brown and dry, the onions are then ready to be cleaned and stored.

Recommended varieties:

*   *Hercules (F^1 hybrid)*
    Large, round onions with a dark golden skin, this variety has a good flavour. It also keeps very well throughout the winter.

- *Hyred (F¹ hybrid)*
  A new hybrid red onion with consistently large crimson bulbs, it does not mature until September. It has a strong, spicy flavour and stores well into the spring in cool, dry conditions.
- *Hytech (F¹ hybrid)*
  Sister to the above, this new hybrid has consistently large golden bulbs that store very well throughout the winter. Its flavour is milder than its red-skinned cousin.
- *Red Baron (AGM)*
  This classic red-skinned onion has a sweet, mild flavour. Each layer of the onion has a red skin, giving an attractive striped effect when it's sliced for salads. Red Baron stores particularly well throughout the winter.
- *White Prince*
  This is a new variety that produces round, pure white bulbs. They have a strong flavour and can be stored into the new year.

Japanese Onions

So-called 'Japanese onions' are useful: they fill the gap between last year's stored onions and the current year's fresh ones. The young bulbs stand well through the winter and get under way again in spring, maturing by June.

Seed facts:

- Sow the seed in August into a bed that is open and sunny.
- The bed should have been thoroughly dug in early winter, incorporating lots of organic matter.
- Before sowing, rake the soil to a fine, even tilth.
- Make a drill with the corner of the rake.
- Sow the onions thinly, replacing the soil with the rake and firming it down with the back.
- Rows should be 30cm (12in) apart.

Maintenance:

- Thin the seedlings to leave them about 15cm (6in) apart.
- Transplant the young bulbs in March if there are gaps in the row.
- If the young bulbs are transplanted, ensure that the roots fall straight down into the planting hole,

leaving the base of the bulb about 1cm (0.4in) below the surface.
- Firm the rows.
- Remove any onion debris to avoid the attentions of onion fly (*see* above, page 113).
- Keep the plants well watered in dry spells.
- Keep them well weeded.
- They should mature from late June onwards.

Recommended varieties:

- *Keepwell (F¹ hybrid)*
  Brown-skinned onions with white flesh that will store into November.
- *Senshyu Semi-Globe*
  This variety produces lots of round, straw-coloured bulbs.

Pickling, Salad/Spring Onions

Spring onions make a marvellous addition to salads and stir-fries. They tend to have a milder flavour than bulb onions and of course they are pulled and eaten much earlier during the summer. There are some very attractive varieties available with red skins. Additionally, there are Italian varieties with elongated bulbs that can be pulled young for salads and the remainder allowed to mature and harvested in August.

Pickling onions are more globe-shaped and can be used instead of shallots in soups and casseroles. These, too, are available in both white- and purple-skinned varieties.

Seed facts:

- Sow spring onions successively from the end of February until mid-April to keep a constant supply for salads.
- Sow them in a sunny, open situation; don't squeeze them in between fast-maturing lettuces, for example.
- Prepare the ground as for sowing Japanese onions (*see* above).

Maintenance:

- Thin the seedlings little and often so that they don't get too congested.

- Make sure the thinnings and debris are removed to keep the onion fly away.
- Keep them well weeded and watered in spells of dry weather.

Recommended varieties:

Spring onions for salads:
- *Crimson Forest*
  These are a very attractive variety with green leaves and dark red stalks. They have a good flavour and look beautiful sliced in a salad. Sow in succession from March until May.
- *Long Red Florence*
  This Italian salad onion can usefully be left to mature for cropping in August. The torpedo-shaped bulbs have a pink-red skin and a mild, sweet taste. Pull them young to eat in salads, or allow them to mature until August. They do not store well.
- *Shimonita*
  This is a Japanese variety with a unique, sweet flavour. If it is thinned to allow the remaining plants a wider space, it will produce thicker stems like a small leek and strongly flavoured, tubular leaves. Sow in succession from February until June.
- *White Lisbon*
  The classic spring onion that is fast-growing, has a silver-white skin and a mild flavour. Sow in succession from March until early May.
- *White Spear (F¹ hybrid)*
  This more decorative spring onion has dark blue-green foliage and straight white stems. It also has a good, mild flavour.

Pickling onions:
- *Paris Silverskin*
  The lovely little silvery globes of this variety are the classic pickling silverskin onion that has been grown commercially for years. Pick them when they are the size of small marbles.
- *Purplette (Cipollini Type)*
  This variety has a decorative purple-red skin like a mini red onion. It turns light pink when pickled. Those that are not harvested for pickling can be left to mature.

Shallots
These little bombs of flavour are no longer just the secret of gourmets. Their mild, sweet flavour is an essential ingredient in traditional French cuisine. From an early planting they mature and are harvested at least a month before onion bulbs: they are far less prone to bolting. Their versatility ensures that if there is not enough room to grow spring onions, pickling onions and full-sized bulbs, shallots will fulfil the function of each. They also store well throughout the winter.

Shallots are a complex of individual bulbs. Each bulb when planted individually will proliferate into six or seven. Larger bulbs are easier to peel for cooking and retain their flavour.

Set facts:

- Plant the bulbs as soon as possible in spring: February to March is ideal.
- Remove the papery tip of the bulbs before planting. This gives the birds less leverage when they try to tug them out.
- Push each bulb into the soil, leaving just the tip showing.
- Space them about 10cm (4in) apart in the rows.
- The rows should be 25cm (10in) apart.
- They should be ready to harvest from early July.

Maintenance:

- Hoe between the rows to keep down the weeds, but take care not to nick the bulbs.
- Keep them watered in dry weather.
- Remove the central bulb when they start to develop in order to make room for the remainder. These mini-bulbs are good in salads.

Recommended varieties:

- *Jermor*
  This is a classic French variety of 'longue' shallot with torpedo-shaped, quite large bulbs. It has an authentic flavour for casseroles and sauces and seems to grow well in the UK.
- *Pensandor*
  This is another classic French 'longue' variety, but with more slender, long bulbs. The flesh is

A bed of shallots.

pink and the skins are dark: an attractive addition to a potager.

- *Picasso*
  This new variety with mild, pink-fleshed shallots is ideal for salads and for pickling. The bulbs mature evenly and early. They are also resistant to bolting.
- *Springfield*
  This variety produces lots of shiny bronze shallots with pink-tinged flesh. It has a strong flavour that is very good in casseroles and soups. It stores especially well.

Other vegetables

These can be placed with the legumes in a three-year rotation.

Courgettes, Pumpkins and Squash (Cucurbits)
Where once the old gardeners only grew giant marrows, these days modern gardeners are well acquainted with courgettes, or zucchini, from France and Italy. And in recent years there has been increasing interest in pumpkins and squashes from the USA.

Choose an essentially sunny spot with plenty of space: pumpkins and squashes have wandering ways, while courgettes sometimes forget they are not sprawling marrows any more. One or two plants will produce enough to feed a family and they are well worth the space they occupy.

Pumpkin.

Common pests and diseases:

- These are remarkably trouble-free and easy vegetables to grow. Towards the end of the summer their leaves tend to become rather mildewed, but this does not seem to affect the fruiting very much.
- Cucumber mosaic virus is a possible complication. The leaves develop pale green patches and the whole plant begins to fail. It's usually spread by aphids. It can also be transmitted from one plant to another by your knife when you cut the fruits. At the first sign it is wise to remove and destroy any infected plants and also to clean your cutting knife with meths.
- But perhaps the riskiest factor is frost. It's essential not to plant out any of the marrow family while there is still a chance of overnight frosts. Seed can be sown in a frost-free greenhouse during April and the young plants hardened off and planted out at the end of May when the garden should be free from the threat of frost. Or sow them outdoors during late April and early May, according to where you live.

Courgettes

These are baby marrows that have been bred to form a more bushy plant and to produce a continuity of small fruit over a long season. Over the past twenty or thirty years they have become so popular that few people grow marrows any more.

There are ball-shaped varieties; yellow-coloured forms; and even striped courgettes. But for the best flavour and texture, pick courgettes small and often, before the flower has fallen off, while they are about 10cm (4in) long. Once they get big, or have wilted in the bottom of the fridge for a couple of days, they become as sappy and tasteless as the ones you buy in the supermarket.

Courgettes are delicious sliced and steamed, fried in olive oil with garlic and lemon zest; grated raw into salad with balsamic vinegar and herbs; or made into soup. Everyone has their own favourite recipe. The bright yellow flowers are also delicious stuffed, dipped in batter and deep-fried.

Seed facts:

- For the maximum cropping period, start the seeds off in a frost-free greenhouse during April.
- Sow two or three seeds to a 5cm (2in) pot at a depth of about 1cm (0.4in).
- Drainage is important: do not use loam-based compost.
- Remove the weakest seedlings as soon as the true leaves emerge.
- Gradually harden them off before planting out at the end of May.
- Alternatively, sow two or three seeds directly from the beginning to middle of May according to your local climate.
- Seeds should take about six to nine days to germinate.
- Prepare planting holes 30cm (12in) cubed.
- Fork over the bottom of the hole and fill it with lots of organic matter.
- Top off with soil mixed with organic fertilizer; this should form a small mound.

Insert a pot next to the main stem to ensure water reaches the roots.

- Plant the young courgette on top of the mound, or sow two or three seeds spaced out at a depth of about 2.5cm (1in). Thin to the strongest when they emerge.
- Insert an empty pot at the top of the mound next to the plant. This is for watering directly into the root system.

Maintenance:

- Keep the plants really well watered in dry weather, as they have a very high water content.
- They may benefit from feeding with a high potash fertilizer such as tomato feed.
- Pick them often; the more they are picked, the more they will produce.

Recommended varieties:

- *Chiaro di Nizza*
  An Italian 'tondo' variety, this courgette is round like a melon. Pick them when they are about the size of tennis balls at the most. The plant has a trailing habit so it could be trained up a wigwam or a fence.
- *Custard White*
  These flat, rounded, scalloped fruits with a white skin look as though they have landed from outer space. They are good to eat either lightly fried with garlic when they are small, or baked whole when they reach maturity.
- *Defender (F¹ hybrid)*
  This bears dark green fruit and has a marked bushy habit that makes it suitable for growing in smaller beds. It is resistant to cucumber mosaic virus.
- *Floridor (F¹ hybrid)*
  The golden globes of this variety will add a puzzling element to your potager.
- *Gold Rush (F¹ hybrid)*
  As yellow as a banana, this is a compact variety that is well suited to an ornamental vegetable garden.
- *Romanesco Latino (F¹ hybrid)*
  The ribs of these fruits are raised and pale, giving it a curiously striped appearance. The ridged effect is very marked when it's sliced up.

- *Rugosa of Friuli*
  An Italian variety from the region around Venice, this is famously knobbly and ugly, but very good to eat.
- *Tuscany (F¹ hybrid)*
  Despite its name, this variety is especially good in colder districts. It produces lots of straight, dark green fruits on a less prickly plant than most. It has been bred for its resistance to powdery mildew.

Pumpkins and Squashes

The recent surge in interest in pumpkins is remarkable. They are very photogenic and so find their way into the gardening magazines. Initially, we grew them to make ghoulish lanterns for Hallowe'en, but increasingly pumpkins are being grown for the kitchen. They are among the few vegetables, or, more correctly, fruit, which have a dual sweet and savoury role in the kitchen. Some, but not all, varieties have well-flavoured seeds too: these are dry-roasted in the oven.

The colours and shapes of pumpkins and squash are very many and various. Some have dense, well-flavoured flesh, while others are best dried and put on the kitchen table for ornament. They mostly store well in a cool, airy, frost-free shed or garage away from the light.

Most pumpkin and squash plants take up a lot more space than courgettes. They trail across the garden, or, if they are suitably supported and not too huge, they can be trained up a fence or wigwam.

Seed and maintenance facts:

- Sow and grow in the same way as courgettes (*see above*).

Recommended varieties:

Pumpkins:
- *Crown Prince*
  This is one of the best pumpkins to grow both for looks and flavour. It has steely blue skin and deep orange flesh. The texture is dense and the flavour is especially good. It also stores well throughout the winter. Its only fault is in its tasteless seeds.

- *Little Gem Rolet*
  This variety produces quantities of small dark green globes the size of tennis balls. They have a good flavour and are produced early in the season.
- *Queensland Blue*
  This is very similar in appearance and taste to Crown Prince, but is slightly smaller and more compact in the garden. The seeds have a better flavour, however.
- *Munchkin*
  A very useful variety for a smaller plot, Munchkin has lots of smaller, bright orange fruits that could quite easily be trained up a wigwam. Each fruit is the ideal size to serve a family at one sitting. It has a good flavour and texture and stores well throughout the winter.

- *Rouge Vif d'Étampes*
  This large variety has deep orange skin, a waxy texture and creamy flavour. It does make a large-growing plant, however, that is more suited to a big garden.
- *Snowman*
  This white-skinned variety has a less dense texture without being watery and a good flavour. The seeds are big and particularly tasty, too.
- *Turk's Turban*
  This is an ornamental variety well worth growing to put in a bowl on the kitchen table and is quite flavoursome, too. Its double globes resemble a blood-orange head sporting an orange and green striped and folded turban.

Pumpkins.

Mini-pumpkin 'Munchkin'.

Florence fennel.

Squashes:

- *Metro (F¹ hybrid)*
  A small butternut squash with the usual hourglass figure, it produces especially sweet flesh and is resistant to powdery mildew.
- *Potimarron*
  This old French variety has a marked chestnut flavour, as its name suggests. It stores well, too.
- *Serpente di Sicilia*
  These Sicilian snakes can grow to about 2m (79in). They are more decorative than tasty, but they look fun trained up through an arch and squirming down to look at you.

Florence Fennel

The bulb-forming fennel is a decorative and delicious addition to an ornamental vegetable garden. Its feathery foliage can be used as a herb, while the distinctive aniseed-flavoured bulbs are a classic accompaniment to fish dishes. They are also excellent grated raw to add a crunch to salads.

Seed facts:

- Sow the seed thinly directly into a prepared seedbed.
- The ground should have been manured for a previous crop.
- Sow between May and July, 38–45cm (15–18in) apart.
- Thin the seedlings when they have made the first true leaves. Don't transplant them.

Maintenance:

- Keep the bed well weeded and watered.

Recommended variety:

- *Orion*
  This variety produces good-sized bulbs in an English summer, whereas some of the other continental varieties fail to heart up.

Sweetcorn

Until comparatively recently it was very difficult to grow sweetcorn successfully in the UK. However, new varieties have been and still are being developed that will produce fat, juicy cobs even in northern parts of the country.

They make a delicious vegetable. New super-sweet varieties are being developed that retain their sweetness for longer after they have been picked; the old varieties tended to turn the sugars into starch very quickly after harvesting. Even so, the sooner the cobs are cooked after picking, the sweeter is the flavour.

To check that a cob is ripe, first look at the tassels: they should have turned brown. Then open the papery jacket and squeeze a kernel between your fingers and thumb. If a milky juice runs out the cob is ripe. If the liquid is watery, the cob is not yet ready. If it is floury the corn is over-ripe. The Italians grind these floury kernels to make polenta.

In recent years 'Super Sweet' varieties have been bred with more plant sugars than usual. It is therefore important to grow different varieties separately to prevent cross-pollination. If these 'Super Sweet' varieties are cross-pollinated with others they may produce much tougher, starchier kernels than you expected.

Chop up the cores of the eaten corn before you put them on the compost heap. The husky, fibrous leaves and stems of the spent plants are also better cut up first too.

Plant out sweetcorn in a grid pattern. It is a form of grass, so it is pollinated by the wind. Close proximity to each other means that the pollen falls from the tassels on to the neighbouring 'flowers' and the cobs are pollinated. (The term 'wind pollination' is misleading: the stems and foliage are too top-heavy for a windy position.)

The soil should have been well manured for a previous crop. Raking in organic fertilizer before planting them out is beneficial. Sowing outdoors is not as successful as starting sweetcorn off in a warm greenhouse, but if necessary a good crop can be achieved from an outdoor sowing in the southern-most counties of the UK.

Common pests and diseases:

- In our cooler climes in the UK sweetcorn is much freer from disease than if it were grown in its native tropical South America.
- Greenfly and aphids in general do sometimes attack the seedlings and young plants.
- If you have mice in your greenhouse when you are sowing they are not averse to stealing the delicious seed.
- In country areas badgers can be quite a nuisance; they love sweetcorn more than tulips.
- Otherwise, the only, quite rare, problem is smut. This is a fungal disease that displays white or pale green growths on the leaves, stems or cobs. If you suspect that your crop has smut, dig it out and destroy all the plants. There is as yet no known treatment.

A stand of sweetcorn.

Seed facts:

- Start the seed off under glass in April. A heated propagator will speed the germination.
- Sow two or three seeds to a 7cm (2¾in) pot.
- In warmer areas of the UK, sow seed outdoors from the middle of May.
- Sow two seeds at 40–45cm (15–18in) intervals in a grid pattern.
- The rows should be 40–45cm (15–18in) apart.
- Seeds should germinate in ten to twelve days.

Maintenance:

- Plant out pot-grown seedlings after hardening them off, at the spacing detailed above.
- Thin the seedlings sown outdoors to leave the stronger of the two.
- Keep the sweetcorn hand-weeded. They are shallow-rooted: hoeing too close to the plant may damage the root systems.
- Cover the roots that may appear at the base of the stems with soil.
- Any side shoots that develop should be left and not removed.
- Ensure that the plants are kept well watered.
- A liquid feed high in potash, such as tomato fertilizer, will improve the cobs.
- They are usually ready to eat from early to mid-September.
- They are not frost-hardy.

Recommended varieties:

- *Mini Pop (F¹ hybrid)*
  This variety has been bred to produce small, tender young corns: there are usually between three and five mini cobs per plant. They should be grown closer together than the other types. Pick them before the tassels appear. They are ideal for stir-fries, or raw in salads.
- *Sundance (F¹ hybrid)*
  This is one of the most reliable sweetcorn varieties for cropping in a poor summer.
- *Sunrise*
  This is a compact variety that can be grown closer together than most, making it ideal for small potager beds.

- *Sweet Nugget (F¹ hybrid)*
  This 'Super Sweet' variety produces long cobs with large yellow kernels with a very sweet flavour. It has been bred to suit cooler conditions.
- *Swift (F¹ hybrid) (AGM)*
  This early 'Super Sweet' variety reliably produces lots of medium-sized cobs with an extra sweet taste. It has been bred especially for the UK climate.
- *Tuxedo*
  This is a tall variety that may require some stout stakes in a windier site. The cobs mature quickly, in about eighty-five days from sowing. It's more tolerant of drought than most other varieties and is also very disease-resistant.

Salads

Most salad vegetables are fast growing and can be popped in after a crop has finished, or while a slower growing vegetable is still small and young (*see* Chapter 7). For this reason, there is no need to prepare the soil beforehand other than to remove the debris of a previous crop thoroughly, weed the area well and rake it over.

Common pests and diseases of salad crops
Slugs and snails are the worst predators of succulent young salad crops, closely followed by rabbits in country gardens. Mildew and damping off can also be a problem if seed is sown too thickly.

Salad rocket is a member of the brassica family. Its worst enemy is the flea beetle, which seems to prefer rocket to almost any other vegetable (*see* above, 'Brassicas and Leafy Vegetables', for ways to tackle flea beetle).

Corn Salad (Lamb's Lettuce)
The great advantage of corn salad is that it produces plenty of cut-and-come-again leaves during the winter. Its taste can be a little bland, but it acts as a foil for stronger-flavoured salad ingredients.

Seed facts:

- Sow in late summer in prepared ground.
- The crop can be protected underneath cloches in colder areas of the UK and during the depths of winter.
- Its leaves can be picked throughout the winter.

Salads in early May.

Recommended variety:

- *Verte de Cambrai*
  This French variety makes small-leaved plants with lots of dark green tender leaves. It tolerates low temperatures well.

Land Cress

This delicious winter salad vegetable has a similar flavour to watercress: nutty and spicy. If grown in succession it will produce leaves from early winter through to the spring.

Seed facts:

- A sowing can be made outside in September in prepared ground.
- Alternatively, it can be sown in a pot in the greenhouse from January onwards.
- It can be picked in eight to ten weeks from sowing.

Lettuce

Lettuces are among the most decorative plants to ornament the vegetable garden. They can be popped

SLUG AND SNAIL CONTROL

Slugs and snails are top of the list of garden pests. In response, the horticultural industry has produced a wealth of deterrents and killers, ranging from:

- organically approved pellets that are not harmful to wildlife or dogs
- nematodes (*Phasmarhabditis hermaphrodita*) that can be applied to particularly vulnerable crops with a watering can
- 'slug pubs' that can be filled with beer and placed where slug-thugs go for a binge
- copper tape to be stuck to the rim of a pot, or placed around individual plants.

Gardeners have also found that:

- coffee grounds are a fairly effective barrier
- crushed oyster shells are very effective used as a barrier; this is sold at agricultural merchants for putting in chicken feed
- slug hunting on a warm, damp evening will reduce the numbers; put the prisoners somewhere far away, so they cannot sneak back later.

A home-made 'slug pub'.

Red and green lettuces surrounded by crushed oyster shells used as an effective slug deterrent.

in between slower growing vegetables and mixed with annual flowers. The ideal soil should contain plenty of organic matter to hold the moisture without becoming boggy. Lettuces grow better in alkaline soil, so if yours is acid, rake in a little lime at a low dose before sowing or planting.

Seed facts:

- Start off an early crop in a frost-free greenhouse at the beginning of March. They hate root disturbance, so they will transplant better from plugs than from a seed tray.
- Thin the seedlings at the true-leaf stage to leave one plant per plug.
- Alternatively, make a shallow drill 1cm (0.4in) deep with the corner of the rake outdoors from March.
- Always sow thinly and little and often.
- Draw the soil back over the drill and tamp it down with the back of the rake.
- Seed will germinate outdoors in seven to twelve days.
- The lettuces in plugs in the greenhouse will be ready to be planted out in April providing the weather is not cold.
- Harden the plug trays off gradually over the course of a week first.
- Unless you live in a cold district, sow a line outside at roughly the same time in March or April; it will take longer to mature.
- Lettuce seed will not germinate well in hot weather: it suffers from heat-induced dormancy.
- Keep unused lettuce seed in its paper packet in a sealed plastic box in the fridge, not in the garden shed.
- Sow successively during cooler weather.
- Lettuce takes between eight and fourteen weeks from sowing to maturity.

Maintenance:

- Thin the seedlings sown outdoors when the first true leaves appear.
- The plants should be about 20–30cm (9–12in) apart.
- Pick them as soon as they start to heart. Cut-and-come-again lettuces can be harvested as soon as they are large enough.

- Once the heart starts to swell upwards the lettuce is beginning to bolt.

Recommended varieties:

- *Bijou (AGM)*
  This red-leaved variety has all the right attributes for an ornamental vegetable garden. It has tasty, cut-and-come-again glossy leaves and it's slow to bolt.
- *Cocarde (AGM)*
  This cut-and-come-again type has large bronze-tipped oak leaves. It's pretty and has a good flavour. A sowing made in the autumn will produce leaves well into the winter with the protection of a cloche.
- *Dazzle*
  With all the crunchy nutty flavour of Little Gem, this variety has shiny red leaves. Each lettuce is just enough for two people and is small enough to be grown more densely than the traditional butterhead varieties.
- *Frillice (AGM)*
  The frilly texture of its loose leaves looks attractive in the potager and its flavour is a good addition to a salad. A July sowing can be harvested as late as early October.
- *Little Gem (AGM)*
  The small, dense heads of this classic dwarf lettuce have an especially good flavour.
- *Parella Green*
  This decorative lettuce makes small, dense heads. It can be sown outdoors in the autumn. Pop a cloche over the plants and they will be ready to eat in January and February.
- *Scarola Verde*
  The large, crunchy heads of this traditional Italian variety are delicious quick-fried with garlic. Sow from June until the end of August in the UK.

Radicchio
The bitter taste of this Italian salad leaf is becoming increasingly popular for its beautiful round heads that resemble beetroot-red lettuces with white midribs. Radicchio will withstand most winters well, except in the colder parts of the UK. The longer-leaved varieties should be tied up for ten days before

picking to blanch them. Try them roasted in olive oil and garlic as a hot vegetable too.

Seed facts:

- Sow seed thinly between mid June and the end of August.
- They will be ready to harvest between September and February.

Recommended varieties:

- *Palla Rossa*
  This classic variety has shiny red globes with white veins to add a crunchy bitterness to winter salads.
- *Palla Rossa Precoce*
  This early form is sown between June and August, to pick from August until November.
- *Rossa Trevigiana Tardiva*
  This traditional late variety makes compact long heads with prominent white veins and ruby-red leaves. It's particularly resistant to frosts. Sow from May until August for picking from October until the end of February.

Radish

Children love to grow this vegetable. It germinates reliably and quickly and produces edible roots just as fast. Its red and white skin looks very pretty, but its flavour is crunchy and peppery. A place in the family potager is a must.

Common pests:

- Radishes can attract flea beetle (*see* above, 'Pests and Diseases of Brassicas and Leafy Vegetables').
- Slugs and snails are also pests; take the usual precautions.

Seed facts:

- Radishes put up with indifferent soil conditions, but will grow much better in a fertile soil that was manured for a previous crop.
- Radishes can be sown from the end of January until August, but the main sowing season is from the end of March until early June. Sow little and often.

- Using the corner of the rake, make a shallow drill about 1cm (0.4in) deep.
- The seeds are big enough for a small child to sow easily, at intervals of about 2.5cm (1in).
- Rake the soil back over the seeds and firm it down with the back of the rake.

Maintenance:

- Thin the seedlings if necessary to leave them about 2.5cm (1in) apart.
- Keep them weeded and watered, especially if the soil is dry.
- They can be harvested as soon as you like, but they become rather woody and fibrous as they get older and larger.

Recommended varieties:

- *French Breakfast (AGM)*
  This is the classic, tubular, red and white radish. It probably grows faster than any other type and has a good flavour.
- *White Icicle*
  This variety produces long white roots. It grows fast and has a particularly sweet flavour.

Salad Rocket

This has to be one of the most popular salad leaves for its distinctive peppery flavour that brings a definite bite to salads and lifts them from the mundane. It may not be particularly pretty, but it takes up little space and is perfect to pop in in between other crops.

Common pests:

- Its one major drawback is its susceptibility to flea beetle (*see* above, 'Pests and Diseases of Brassicas and Leafy Vegetables'). Plants can be protected with fleece if this proves to be a major problem, although fleece is not very ornamental.

Seed facts:

- Sow in succession from March until October.
- Rocket takes about eight weeks from sowing to produce edible leaves.

- Sow seed thinly in drills 1–2.5cm (0.4 1in) deep.
- Sow little and often to produce a succession.
- Cut the leaves regularly to prevent bolting and the development of tough outer leaves.

Recommended varieties:

- *Apollo*
  This fast-growing variety produces lots of tender, rounded leaves with plenty of pepperiness without bitterness.
- *Turkish Rocket*
  This is a variety that claims to be more resistant to flea beetle than the ordinary type.
- *Wild Rocket*
  The wild form has darker and more deeply divided leaves with a stronger flavour.

Sorrel

The cultivated form of this native plant has a sharp and lemony tang to taste. Its young leaves can be added to salads, or they can be made into a delicious cold soup.

Seed facts:

- Sorrel is a perennial herb.
- Sow it in draining soil from March.

Recommended variety:

- *Blood Veined*
  The emerald green leaves have shining red stalks and red veins, making it an attractive addition to any potager.

Potatoes

Growing enough spuds to feed an entire family requires plenty of space and so potatoes really only warrant inclusion in the smaller beds of a potager if they are special.

Traditionally, potatoes were grown as a pioneer crop in new vegetable beds: they seem to clean the soil of many pests and diseases. Also the whole business of planting them and progressively earthing them up means that any residual weed roots are

Buckler-leaved Sorrel.

Potatoes grown in large containers and recycled compost bags.

regularly removed. But after a few years potato blight inevitably breaks out and those beds then become unsuitable for potato growing.

However, many gardeners grow a small crop of a special variety in a large pot. Clean commercial compost is used each time, so the soil does not become contaminated. If the crop does get blight then it's easy to dispose of the entire plant, pot and all. But it's important that you act quickly before the blight transfers to other potato pots or the tomatoes.

Growing facts:

- When the tubers arrive from the seed merchant, sit them in open egg boxes with their buds upmost. Put the boxes somewhere light and frost-free until they begin to sprout.
- Plant two or three tubers at double their depth in 20ltr (35pt) containers half-filled with commercial compost. Keep the pots somewhere light and frost-free.
- As the top growth extends add more compost, until the whole pot is full.
- When the frosts are over, it's safe to place them outside somewhere sunny.

Recommended varieties for pot growing:

- *Anya*
  This salad potato has been bred from the delicious, but far too knobbly Pink Fir Apple. It has a dense, waxy texture with an even better flavour. From a March planting it can be harvested from July. It has a fairly good disease resistance.
- *Arran Victory*
  This is an old maincrop variety that has been brought out of retirement by popular demand for its purple flesh and fine flavour. It's quite floury, so microwave or steam it rather than boil it. It's also fairly disease-resistant.
- *Sante*
  This maincrop variety has a good resistance to blight, scab and eelworm (*see* Chapter 7).
- *Valor*
  This is another highly resistant variety that crops quite late in the season. It is very prolific, so plant only one or, at most, two per container.

TENDER VEGETABLE VARIETIES TO GROW UNDER PROTECTION

If there is room for a greenhouse you can grow a much wider range of summer vegetables. If the greenhouse is heated to provide frost protection, this widens the scope even more. But a greenhouse is not essential for growing tender vegetables.

Many of the seed companies now supply young plants in plugs that have already been raised under glass: a short cut for those without a greenhouse. These plugs can be potted up and kept on a sunny window sill, or in a conservatory or porch until all risk of frost has passed. The young plants can then be gradually hardened off and planted into growing bags, or, more decoratively, into large terracotta pots in a sunny position out of the wind. Use good proprietary compost and keep them well fed with tomato fertilizer throughout the growing season.

Some of the more tender vegetables need an extra long growing season that can best be provided under glass. And given the extra protection of a greenhouse from the wind and rain of our British summers, these vegetables are much more productive and their quality is much improved.

Common pests and diseases
Pests and diseases are more plentiful too with such a luxurious upbringing, so extra attention needs to be paid to their prevention. Yellow sticky papers are hung in the greenhouse, not for decoration, nor just to trap flying predators, but in order to monitor exactly what is on the loose inside your greenhouse. Inspect the papers regularly and you may be able to head off a deadly attack of whitefly, red spider mite, aphids and the rest. You will need to be extra vigilant for fungal diseases, too. Damping-off disease can rampage through your seedlings in hours on a warm spring day.

There are chemical sprays that will go some way to sorting out most of these troubles if you can catch them early, but simple greenhouse hygiene is one of the best preventatives. If your plants are affected and you do choose the pesticide route, use a different chemical every time, otherwise the pest or disease will build up a resistance to that chemical and it will no be longer effective. No one should have a 'favourite' pesticide.

Organic methods are also extremely effective (*see* Chapter 10). However, it's usually not possible to mix chemical with organic: it's no good spraying insecticide in a greenhouse full of predatory wasps. They will die, too.

Aubergine

Aubergines used only to be grown in warmer countries and although seed was available in the UK, often our summers were not long enough to produce more than one or two stunted fruit a year. But the UK plant breeders have worked to create aubergines that are more than tolerant of cooler conditions, and which will crop well in our shorter summers.

Aubergine 'Long Purple'.

There are several different shapes, sizes and colours of aubergines that the amateur gardener can now grow successfully from seed. And that they are decorative is without doubt.

Common pests and diseases:

- Perhaps the worst pest is whitefly. This seems to target aubergine plants from the seedling stage. Within the greenhouse the best recourse is to use predatory wasps (*see* Chapter 10). If the infestation is severe it may be wiser to destroy the plants altogether, clean the greenhouse thoroughly and grow something else for the rest of the year.

Seed facts:

- Sow seeds in February in a temperature of 16–18°C (60–65°F). A heated propagator with a thermostat is ideal.
- Put two or three seeds to each 7cm (2¾in) pot of commercial compost.
- They should germinate in seven to ten days.

Maintenance:

- Thin the seedlings at the first true-leaf stage to leave just one per pot.
- Keep the pots either in a frost-free greenhouse, or somewhere cool and light such as a porch or conservatory.
- Once the danger of frost has passed, they can be hardened off and planted outside in a terracotta pot somewhere warm, sunny and protected from the wind.
- They could also be transplanted when they have filled their pots into growing bags, three to a bag and kept inside the greenhouse.
- They will need staking: the aubergine fruits will make the plants top heavy.
- Keep them well watered.
- Feed the plants every ten to fourteen days with tomato fertilizer from the time the flowers start setting fruit.
- They will be ready to pick from August onwards.

Recommended varieties:

- *Bonica (F¹ hybrid)*
  This is a high-yielding variety especially suitable for growing in containers. It is compact and

bushy, with the fruits forming early and setting well.

- *Long Purple*
  The elongated, shiny purple fruits make this a most attractive variety. It has a good flavour too.
- *Moneymaker (F¹ hybrid)*
  A prolific variety, this has been bred to produce fruits earlier and more quickly than most.
- *Snowy*
  As its name suggests, these fruits are white and shiny. They make a decorative alternative to the purple forms.

Capsicum

This family includes chillies and sweet peppers. They are as easy to grow in a greenhouse as tomatoes and have similar needs. Peppers are not hardy plants, yet they need to be started off early to give a long growing season in order for them to ripen fully. A sunny window sill, porch or conservatory could take the place of a greenhouse and they can be successfully grown outside in a sunny position that is away from the wind.

Common pests and diseases:

- In common with most greenhouse crops, all members of the capsicum family are susceptible to whitefly and greenfly. Once these have been detected, take the appropriate steps as with aubergines (*see* above).

Seed facts:

- Sow seeds in plugs, peat pots or 7cm (2¾in) plastic pots. Put two seeds to each pot or plug.
- Put them in a heated propagator set at 17°C (63°F) in February or March, either in the greenhouse or on the window sill.
- The seeds should germinate in about seven to ten days.

Sweet bell peppers.

Maintenance:

- Thin to a single, healthy seedling as soon as possible.
- Gradually reduce the temperature to about 14–15°C (57–59°F).
- When the seedlings have filled their plugs or pots, transplant them into larger pots to keep them moving.
- Towards the end of May they should be in their final pots or growing bags.
- Alternatively, if the plants are to be grown outdoors, harden them off before planting out.
- Outdoor plants should be set about 50cm (20in) apart.
- Pinch out the growing tip when the plants are about 30cm (12in) tall in order to make them bush out.
- Feed them with half-strength, high-potash liquid tomato food, at the intervals recommended on the bottle.

Cucumbers.

- Sweet peppers should be ready to pick from August. Chilli peppers need to be ripened for longer: the more hot sunshine they receive, the hotter they are.

Cucumbers

A greenhouse full of cucumbers is an amazing sight in August. However, unless you run a market garden one plant is more than sufficient for most family needs. Their green colour, refreshing taste and crisp texture can be used not just in salads and the legendary sandwiches, but when combined with tomatoes, cucumbers make delicious cold soups and can even be stir-fried.

The old gardening books would advise that cucumbers and tomatoes do not grow well together: they need different conditions. However, in practice, modern varieties seem happy to put up with their red neighbours.

Remove the male flowers before the bees get to work pollinating the females: pollinated fruits contain larger seeds and have a poor, slightly bitter flavour. Female flowers are easy to spot: they have embryonic fruits behind the yellow flowers. All-female F^1 hybrids relieve modern gardeners of this job: they only occasionally produce male flowers when conditions are poor.

Cucumber plants will need tying in to a 2m (79in) stake. When the fruits start to develop they may also need some extra tying in, so as to support their weight.

Cucumbers can also be grown outdoors in exactly the same way as other members of the marrow family. However, they are somewhat more susceptible to the attentions of slugs and snails close to the ground, so choose a climbing variety and one that is specifically for growing outdoors.

Common pests and diseases:

- Cucumbers are susceptible to all the usual suspects in a greenhouse, including powdery mildew.
- Whitefly are the most common problem. If they are spotted early you could resort to chemical sprays on young plants. Alternatively, predatory wasps could be introduced (*see* Chapter 10).
- Cucumber mosaic virus could also be a problem. If pale patches develop on the leaves remove the

affected plants and destroy them. It's wise to choose a disease-resistant variety.

Seed facts:

- Select only the fattest seeds and don't sow too many. They will occupy sought-after space in a heated greenhouse or on your window sill, only to be thrown on to the compost heap.
- Sow the seeds on their edges.
- Sow two seeds to each 7cm (2¾in) pot in mid-February in a heated propagator.
- Set the thermostat to 20°C (68°F).
- The seed should germinate in about three to five days.

Maintenance:

- Thin the seedlings down to singletons when their true leaves appear.
- Maintain the same minimum temperature either in the greenhouse or on a sunny window sill.
- Pot on the seedlings into a good proprietary compost as soon as their roots fill the pots. Increase the pot size a stage at a time. The final pot size should be at least 3ltr (5pt).
- Once the temperatures have warmed up in spring and the young plants get larger, the thermostat can be reduced in the greenhouse. Those grown on a window sill can be brought into a frost-free greenhouse.
- As the cucumber plants extend, train them into a cane or a wire tied into the frame of the green-house. Side shoots should also be supported.
- Once they start to flower, pinch out the tips of the side shoots to leave two leaf joints past the flower.
- Keep the soil moist, not wet. And keep the air as moist, yet well ventilated, as possible.
- Begin feeding with tomato fertilizer once the young fruits begin to swell.
- Pick them young for maximum flavour and to keep them coming.
- If the cucumbers become pale and yellow they will prevent the plant from producing any more fruit. These mature cucumbers are not good to eat, either.

Recommended varieties:

- *Euphya (F¹ hybrid)*
  This is one of the best all-female hybrids that have been bred for disease resistance. It's prolific and the cucumbers have a good flavour.
- *Cucino (F¹ hybrid)*
  This is a new variety that produces lots of mini-cucumbers, which may prove more useful than long, slicing forms. It's an all-female hybrid. It sets well in hot spells and is tolerant of powdery mildew.
- *Passandra (F¹ hybrid)*
  This variety makes shorter, 15cm (6in) long fruit, which might also prove more practical in the kitchen. It's another all-female hybrid and has a good resistance to downy and powdery mildews, as well as mosaic virus.

Chilli Peppers

The tremendous rise in popularity of chillies has resulted in a similarly increased interest in growing

Chilli peppers.

them at home. They are highly decorative in the greenhouse, so decorative that the temptation is to grow more than one or two plants. If you have overenthused, they do freeze very well and can be used straight from the freezer in curries and hot Thai and Mexican food. There are so very many ways to use chillies in cooking that you may even find you need to grow more of them each year.

Each chilli pepper has a slightly different flavour, if you can get past its heat. A rule of thumb is that the smaller the fruit, the hotter it is. If you prefer your chillies a little less hot, remove the seeds before cooking with them. Take care when you handle chillies not to touch your eyes, or any other delicate part of your anatomy. They bite! If they get you, wash well with cold water to relieve the heat. And if you eat them too hot, drink something sweet. Water does not help.

To get the greatest heat from your chillies, they need to be grown at high temperatures. So if you don't have a greenhouse, choose a sunny kitchen window sill, porch or conservatory. If you do grow them outside, bring them indoors at the end of the summer so that they can ripen thoroughly. The riper they are, the hotter.

Hot chilli peppers are not just red when they are ripe; they are black, yellow and pale green too. So, one or two plants of different colours would really cheer up the kitchen window sill. And instead of freezing all the surplus chillies, make an orange and red string of them to hang in the kitchen. They retain much of their heat when dried.

Recommended varieties:

- *Apache*
  This dwarf bushy variety produces lots of small fruit that get hotter as they ripen.
- *Big Sun*
  Although it resembles a miniature sweet pepper, Big Sun packs a very hot punch. It dries well too.
- *Caldero*
  This is another compact variety whose medium hot chillies turn from creamy yellow to orange and red. It makes an attractive plant for a pot on the garden table.
- *Habanero*
  This fiery variety is used in West Indian cooking.

- *Hot Mexican*
  This is one of the hottest chillies, with lots of small, thin fruit carried on a dwarf plant. It dries well, too.
- *Jalapeno*
  This is a traditional, blunt-nosed variety with a little less fire.

Sweet Peppers

Sweet or bell peppers are even easier to grow than chillies. They will produce plenty of fruit if they are planted outdoors too. Their shiny red, orange, yellow and green fruits are highly decorative in the potager, or growing in pots outside or in the greenhouse. Modern varieties are prolific and develop well in UK summers.

They need no introduction as a vegetable for putting in salads, casseroles, stir-fries and for stuffing and baking.

Recommended varieties:

- *Arianne (F^1 hybrid) (AGM)*
  These rounded bell peppers are green when young, maturing to a rich orange with a crisp, sweet flavour. They are an easy and reliable variety to grow.
- *Atris (F^1 hybrid) (AGM)*
  This variety has a long, tapering shape called an ox horn, with a thick skin and a mild sweet flavour. It's a very decorative variety that ripens from green to a dark, shining red. It has been bred to produce a prolific number of fruits on a single plant.
- *Mavras (AGM)*
  These fruits turn deep purple and finally red when they are mature. They would look good in any situation. Mavras produces fruit earlier in the summer than others.
- *Ringo*
  This is another ox-horn variety with sunny yellow fruits up to 15cm (6in) in length. It has a good flavour and would blend decoratively with any of the other varieties.
- *Topepo Rosso (F^1 hybrid)*
  This and the next variety resemble large tomatoes rather than bell peppers. Their size and shape make them ideal for stuffing and baking.

Ox-horn peppers.

- *Topepo Giallo (F¹ hybrid)*
  The golden equivalent of Topepo Rosso, this variety is high yielding and equally good for stuffing and baking. These two would make an attractive, if puzzling, pair.

Tomatoes

In a hot summer, tomatoes can be grown really successfully outside, but they need to be started off inside in March or April and weather forecasters tend not to predict what sort of summer we will experience so far ahead. By the time tomato plants need space in a cold greenhouse it has usually been vacated by the earlier crops, so it makes sense if you have a greenhouse, whether heated or not, to opt to grow indoor tomatoes.

In the kitchen, tomatoes are, of course, an essential ingredient in countless dishes. But it's hard to beat the taste and smell of a freshly picked tomato without any trimmings. Usually, tomato growers experience a glut in August and September, but there are plenty of recipes for soups and sauces to use them up. Or, if they are first fried with chopped onions, garlic and basil, they make a delicious sauce that freezes well. At the end of the season green tomatoes will ripen in a bowl of bananas, as these give off the right gases to encourage ripening.

For a long time, tomatoes were bred for exhibition with scant regard for flavour. Now, however, most gardeners choose them for their taste and looks. The small-fruiting varieties are often the sweetest and some are small enough to plant in a large pot on the garden table to nibble *al fresco*. Yellow-fruited tomatoes are also among the tastiest and would look attractive growing alongside the red varieties in the greenhouse. Then there are striped ones, purple ones and orange ones too. The large 'beef' tomatoes are rather coarser and in the UK they tend not to have as good a flavour as those bought in an Italian market on holiday. Plum tomatoes are thinner skinned and also have a good flavour. And if you go on-line, there are all sorts of different varieties to tempt you.

Tomatoes are a very attractive crop growing in a greenhouse alongside a cucumber plant, some peppers and maybe an aubergine or two. On a dreary wet summer day it is a great pleasure to spend some time in the greenhouse removing their side shoots and breathing their distinctive scent. They are grown either as a single stem or a bush. The single stem varieties tend to produce fewer, larger tomatoes. They need the side shoots removing every few days while they are growing. The bush-grown types do not need the side shoots pinching out. They produce lots of smaller tomatoes. Once the fifth truss has set on either a bush or a single-stemmed plant, remove the growing tip about two leaf joints from the topmost truss. If the plant carries on producing more trusses the fruits will all be smaller and less juicy and you will end up with a lot of small green bullets at the end of the season.

Common pests and diseases:

All the usual suspects – greenfly, whitefly and mildew – affect tomato plants. In addition, there is a host of problems specific to tomatoes. If you

Tomato 'Gardener's Delight'.

worried about them all you would never grow tomatoes in the first place. Some of the more common are:

- **Blossom end rot** If you do not water the plants regularly and allow them to dry out, the fruits can develop a brown patch on the base opposite the stem.
- **Mosaic virus** This presents similar symptoms to cucumber mosaic virus, with pale mottled patches on the leaves. The remedies are equally dire (*see* 'Cucumber', above).
- **Splitting** This is also due to irregular watering. Pick the fruits as soon as they colour, before the cracks become mouldy.
- **Tomato blight** Related to potato blight, this disease can be transmitted from one vegetable to the other. The leaves start to wilt and turn brown, so it quickly becomes apparent what the problem is. If it affects your plants remove and destroy them. Prevent blight by growing tomatoes at a distance from potatoes and ensure that any tomato debris is cleared away in the greenhouse. Use mains water for irrigation, not from a butt. If you identify the problem early you could use a fungicidal spray.
- **Tomato leaf curl** Sometimes the leaves become distorted but remain otherwise green and healthy. This particular disorder can be lived with. It does not tend to affect the fruits.

Seed facts:

- Sow two or three seeds in each 7cm (2¾in) pot at a depth of about 1cm (0.4in).
- Keep them at a minimum temperature of 16°C (61°F). A heated propagator is useful, or a warm kitchen window sill.
- Use commercial compost.
- Don't sow seed too early, or the young plants will be drawn up with long gaps between the leaf nodes due to the lower levels of light in early spring. Late March or early April is soon enough.
- The seed should start to germinate in eight to eleven days.

Maintenance:

- Thin the seedlings to leave the strongest when they have made a pair of true leaves.

- They can be grown on at a cooler temperature: 10–15°C (50–59° F).
- Pot them on in stages as their roots fill each pot. Potting them directly into a large pot will cause the roots to hug the sides of the pot, leaving wet compost underneath the centre of each plant. The final container should be a 5ltr (9pt) pot, or plant them three to a growing bag.
- When the young plants are in their final container tie the main stem loosely to a cane, or wind a string around the stem, run it up vertically and tie it in to the frame of the greenhouse roof firmly. It will have to bear the weight of all the tomatoes and the plant eventually.
- Bush tomatoes will not need such elaborate staking, but they do benefit from a few canes to prevent the plant from collapsing under the weight of its fruit.
- Bush tomatoes usually stop growing when they are 30–38cm (12–15in) tall.
- Start feeding the plants with tomato fertilizer as directed on the bottle once they are in their final containers.
- In dry weather spray the flowers with clean water to help them to set. You could also tap their canes to disperse the pollen, although this is not entirely necessary.
- The fruit should start ripening from mid-August and continue until October.
- Nip out the shoots as they appear in the stem and leaf joints unless they are bush tomatoes.
- Take out the growing tip, leaving two leaves above the topmost truss when the plant has set a maximum of five trusses.
- Keep the greenhouse well ventilated throughout the summer.

Recommended varieties:

- *Fantasio (F¹ hybrid)*
  This variety bears lots of large, heavy fruit with a good flavour. It has been bred for its resistance to tomato blight.
- *Gardener's Delight (AGM)*
  This is one of the most popular varieties developed in recent years, and deservedly so. It produces an abundance of small, sweet tomatoes with a terrific flavour.

Tomatoes 'Tumbling Tom'.

- *Gartenperle*
  This is another deliciously sweet cherry tomato that is recommended for growing in a window box, pot or hanging basket.
- *Golden Sweet (F¹ hybrid)*
  This new golden orange variety has an especially good flavour. It's very prolific and the plant is disease-resistant.

- *Harlequin (F¹ hybrid)*
  This decorative red variety has upturned calyxes like a little hat. Its plum-shaped fruit is exceptionally sweet and juicy.
- *Tigerella (AGM)*
  This is a striped variety that certainly adds a zing to the greenhouse and zest to a salad with its tangy flavour. It's prolific and early to bear fruit.

- *Tumbling Tom Yellow*
  Like Gartenperle, this variety is excellent for window boxes and hanging baskets, but its fruits are orange-yellow.

PERMANENT VEGETABLES

If there is room in your ornamental vegetable garden for permanent vegetables, there are a few that are both decorative and delicious. The soil will need to be well dug beforehand and plenty of organic matter incorporated initially. Thereafter, a sterile mulch such as ornamental grade bark or grit will help to keep the weeds down and gradually improve the soil.

Artichokes

Globe Artichokes
There can be no doubt that globe artichokes are an elegant and dramatic addition to any part of the garden. Their relatives, the cardoons, are more usually grown amongst the flowers, and of course their young leaves can also be eaten.

The young silver foliage of both cardoons and globe artichokes emerges very early in the spring and by July those globes that are left uneaten burst into thistle-like flowers that are very attractive to bees and butterflies.

Globe artichokes prefer a free-draining soil and full sun. In colder parts of the UK they may well prove non-hardy, especially in a wet winter. Their leaves are very big and could swamp anything growing within a radius of at least a metre, including a neat box hedge. So position them well away from anything they could overwhelm. Seed strains of globe artichokes mostly come true; alternatively buy young plants of named varieties if you can get hold of them.

The traditional method of preparing artichokes is to clip off the spines from the tips of the leaves, cut back the coarse stem to the base of the globe, and boil them for thirty to forty-five minutes. Pull each leaf off from the outside in, dip the end in melted butter and chew off the buttery flesh. Eventually all that is left is the 'choke'. Pull the hairs

off the base plate and remove any tough bits of stalk, then pour the remainder of the melted butter in the middle and eat it with a knife and fork. It's not a meal, it's an experience.

Common pests and diseases:

- Artichokes are relatively free from pests and diseases. Perhaps the only nuisance would be from a few slugs overwintering in the crown.

Seed facts:

- Sow a named seed strain in a cold greenhouse in February to March.
- Sow two or three seeds to a 7cm (2¾in) pot and thin them to leave the strongest at the true-leaf stage.

Globe artichokes.

- Alternatively, in warmer districts they can be sown outdoors in April.
- Choose a well-drained, sunny position.

Maintenance:

- Pot on into increasingly larger pots.
- Overwinter the pots under cold glass to keep them on the dry side of damp.
- Alternatively, thin the outdoor-grown seedlings to about 10cm (4in) apart in April.
- Transplant them to their permanent positions the following April.
- They should be spaced at least 1m (39in) apart in their final positions.

Recommended varieties:

- *Emerald*
  This is a good variety to try in cooler areas of the UK. It has fleshy leaves and hearts with a good nutty flavour. If it is started off early in the greenhouse in February it may well produce heads in its first year.
- *Green Globe*
  This large-fruited variety produces plenty of round heads. Protect the crowns with a mulch or straw in early winter in colder areas of the UK.
- *Purple Globe – Romanesco*
  The heads of this variety are attractively tinged red-purple. They are slightly smaller and the plant is shorter than the other two varieties, but it's somewhat hardier for growing in cooler areas.

Jerusalem Artichokes

Although they have a distinctly similar flavour to globe artichokes, the two plants are not related. This sunflower relative produces tubers below the ground like a potato. It's tall and very hardy, erupting in small yellow sunflowers in late summer.

Jerusalem artichokes are delicious made into a soup, or just boiled or roasted with Sunday lunch. Their tubers can be rather knobbly to peel. As you peel them, drop them into water with a few drops of vinegar to stop them discolouring.

Common pests and diseases:

- There seems to be very little that interferes with Jerusalem artichokes.

Tuber facts:

- Plant the tubers when you receive them from the seed merchant, about 38–45cm (15–18in) apart at a depth of about 12.5cm (5in).

Maintenance:

- Earth them up when they are about 30cm (12in) tall.
- They will reach over 1.5m (60in) in height.
- Harvest them during the winter months as you need them.

Recommended variety:

- *Fuseau*
  This has larger and smoother tubers that are much easier to peel.

Asparagus

The airy foliage of asparagus is so pretty that it's used by florists and flower arrangers. It sparkles in the rain and the occasional bright orange berries are like jewels.

Asparagus is one of the most delicious spring vegetables of all. To prepare it, cut the spears at soil level and wash off the soil. Holding the tip between finger and thumb in one hand and the cut end in the other, bend the spear down until it snaps. Discard the fibrous lower end. Then, there is really nothing to beat simply steaming the spears and serving them with melted butter and brown bread.

Asparagus is easy and trouble-free to grow and well worth waiting three or four years for the crowns to develop sufficiently before the spears can be picked. However tempting it may be to pick them sooner, it is essential that the plant gets established and builds up a good crown before you cut off what are the emerging young shoots. They can be harvested from spring until June. Thereafter, picking them only serves to weaken the plant and reduce the following year's crop. Allow the plant to develop its typical lacy foliage all summer and die down with the first frosts.

Buy named crowns from a reputable seed merchant; they will be delivered in time to plant them. Growing asparagus from seed means it will take much longer before you can harvest the spears and their quality will be variable. Some of the plants will be female: these are considered inferior in quality and less prolific. So it's not worth the wait of growing from seed.

Common pests and diseases:

Problems with growing asparagus are rare, but there are one or two conditions that might affect your asparagus bed:

- **Violet root rot:** This is a fungal disease that causes the yellowing of the fronds in circular patches in the summer before the plant dies down. If you inspect the soil you may see violet-coloured threads running through the roots. This can spread to affect other root vegetables. The best remedy is to dig out all the asparagus crowns permanently, taking care not to shake off the infected soil. Then find a different location to grow fresh asparagus crowns. There are no resistant varieties and no known remedy.

Sparkling asparagus leaves.

Fresh young asparagus shoots.

- **Asparagus rust:** This manifests itself as bright red-orange spots on the foliage. The spores overwinter in the soil and reinfect the shoots as they emerge in spring. It can also affect onions. Again, the remedy is drastic: remove and destroy the plants and do not replant asparagus in the same place.
- **Asparagus beetle:** A beautiful red, yellow and brown insect, with insignificant grey grubs, the asparagus beetle is quite easy to spot and remove and squash. The grubs eat the leaves for a few weeks, then pupate down in the soil ready to re-emerge next year. Clear up the dead foliage at the end of every year and keep the bed clear of debris and stones where the pupae may be concealed. Rotenone spray is effective and acceptable to organic growers if the beetles become a problem, but usually they are more of a nuisance than a curse.

Growing facts:

- Dig an asparagus bed well over the winter and incorporate plenty of organic matter in the lower spit.
- Plant the crowns as soon as they arrive, ensuring that the roots are well covered and the buds are just below the surface.
- Add organic matter every winter after clearing away the faded stems.

Recommended varieties:

- *Backlim (F¹ hybrid) (AGM)*
  This all-male variety has large spears with tightly closed tips. It's also disease-resistant.
- *Gijnlim (F¹ hybrid) (AGM)*
  This is another all-male variety with closed purple tips. It has an especially good flavour.

- *Stewarts Purple*
  This is a new purple variety with long, tender and especially sweet spears. The colour is retained if they are steamed and they are good in salads. Stewarts Purple can be cut as early as the end of April.

Seakale

Related to the brassicas, seakale is a perennial, native to the UK. It can still be seen growing on cliffs by the sea. It would be rather too tough and chewy for modern palates to eat as a vegetable, but with the aid of a terracotta forcing pot it can be blanched. The shoots are best steamed and served with melted butter like asparagus. And seakale is a beautiful plant with its glossy blue-purple leaves once the terracotta forcer is removed.

Growing facts:

- Allow the plant to get established and grow for a full year.
- In winter clear away all the plant debris and in January or February, before the shoots start to push up, cover the crown entirely with a rhubarb forcer with a lid, or an old bucket. Make sure that the light cannot get in so that the shoots stay white.
- By March or April, when they are about 20–25cm (8–10in) tall, the delicate white shoots are ready for harvesting. It may be difficult to resist the temptation to pick all the shoots, but leave some for the plant to regrow.

Recommended variety:

- *Angers*
  This variety has been selected because it produces more stems than the usual. Seed merchants normally deliver the 'thongs' during the spring.

CHAPTER 9

What to grow – flowers and herbs

Once you have chosen vegetable seed from the long list of both decorative, and also perhaps favourite but not so decorative vegetables, it's time to consider which flowers and herbs you would like to grow with them.

All flowers add to the intrinsic beauty of the vegetables, but in an ornamental vegetable garden they contribute something extra: pizzazz. Many summer flowers rejoice in strong, hot colours that complement the purples, oranges and ruby reds of kale, cabbages, pumpkins, Swiss chard and beetroot. Others have gentler colours in the pink, mauve and blue spectrum. These also complement the purples: French beans, red cabbages, sprouting broccoli. And they blend well with the greens of peas, lettuces and winter cabbages. Often it is these softer colours that predominate in spring and early summer. Pansies, pinks, daisies (*Bellis*) and many other small flowers complement the burgeoning green seedlings and the last of the winter vegetables.

Some flowers are useful companion plants to certain vegetables (*see* Chapter 10). Others encourage bees and butterflies to pollinate those vegetable flowers that need cross-fertilization. And of course, some herbs and flowers are as delicious to eat as lettuce and rocket. Flowers for picking are also more usefully grown alongside the vegetables: there's no need to worry about leaving a hole in your summer borders if you pick the head off a sunflower, or a bunch of snapdragons for the house. Some flowers are ideal to grow for drying in bunches and decorating the house in winter. Pick them before they are fully open and hang them upside down in bunches somewhere cool, dark and airy: the garage would be ideal. Many of these 'everlasting' flowers need much poorer, dryer soil than the vegetables. It might even be worth considering making a special area or setting aside a dedicated bed for them.

The list of flowers and herbs below is divided primarily into seasons and further into colours. Their properties and uses are also outlined.

SPRING

Reds and pinks

*Daisy (*Bellis perennis*) (perennial)*
The cultivated cousin of the lawn daisy is a typical cottage garden plant. The cultivars are usually double in shades of apple-blossom pink and white. Although *Bellis* is generally sold as a spring bedding plant, it is perennial, albeit rather short-lived. Its flowers have been eaten since Elizabethan times and look pretty decorating a spring salad of young leaves.

Instead of buying trays of plants sold for spring bedding, *Bellis* could easily be raised from seed sown in spring and planted out in the summer to flower the following spring. It prefers the same rich soil as vegetables and would make a very good edging plant for formal beds. Pick off the dead heads regularly; this will encourage them to flower again at the end of the summer.

*Pinks (*Dianthus*) (perennial)*
The silvery foliage of garden pinks would also make a good edging, especially for dryer soils in full sun.

Tulips and wallflowers.

There are numerous cultivars, both 'old' and modern. The older varieties, although they only flower once, have a better scent.

Historically, pinks were dunked in tankards of hot wine to impart the flavour of cloves to the brew, hence 'clove pinks' and the old name 'Sops in Wine'. The older cultivars tend to be in shades of white, ruby red and the eponymous pink. Look out for the beautiful 'old laced' pinks with deep red edges to the petals.

Buy the named cultivars as young plants, or raise annual bedding pinks from seed sown in spring and planted out in summer.

Sweet William (biennial)
Related to pinks and carnations, Sweet Williams are usually grown as a biennial. They are bigger and coarser, with green leaves and fascinating red, pink and white flowers with contrasting eyes and markings. There's even a stunning dark velvet-maroon variety. Sweet Williams are tougher and happier than pinks in less well-drained soil.

Buy them as young plants in autumn to flower the following year, or sow the seed in May and plant them out in summer where they are to flower the following year.

Tulips (bulb)

Tulips make a dramatic statement in any garden: they bring a potager to life in spring. Plant the bulbs in autumn at twice their own depth in full sun and draining soil. Once the flowers have faded, snap off the seed cases and lift the whole plant. Dry them off in a warm greenhouse or garage and when the leaves have totally desiccated, clean them up and store them in net bags where the mice cannot reach them. They will have made small bulblets by the autumn when they can all be replanted to flower the following spring.

Blues and purples

Heartsease (Viola tricolor) (annual)

Little Heartsease or Johnny-Jump-Ups are delightful used either as an edging plant or allowed to seed into places they know they should not. And they are delicious tossed into a green salad. Their seed could either be scattered where you want them to grow, or they could be started off more formally in seed trays in spring and planted out later in the summer. They only need planting once. They will invariably pop up each year unless you are ruthless with the hoe.

Pansies and other violas are less likely to seed true, but they could also be found a home amongst the vegetables. Winter pansies could cheer up the parsnips and leeks from September to April; they are very pretty in a little brown jug, too.

Rosemary (Rosmarinus officinalis) (hardy shrub)

One of the most venerated herbs both medicinally and in cooking, rosemary was brought to these shores by the Romans. It therefore prefers the sun and good drainage that it would enjoy in its native Mediterranean. Its clear blue flowers appear early in spring and often repeat later in a warm autumn.

Rosemary grows into a small woody shrub. Its growth can get quite beautifully gnarled and twisted

from year to year, but it is quite short-lived. Trim back the branches after it has finished flowering to keep it more compact. After about five or six years it would be wise to take cuttings in readiness for its demise. Side shoots rooted in spring can be potted up and planted out the following spring.

Sage (Salvia officinalis) (hardy shrub)

This is another beautiful sub-shrub that came with the Romans from the Mediterranean, so it too prefers full sun and good drainage. Its lavender flowers appear in spring and attract the bees, as does the herb rosemary.

Once the flowers are finished cut the stems in half, back to a new shoot and the plant will stay lower and more mounding. The new leaves can be dried for use either at this stage or later in the summer. The cuttings can be rooted to replace the original after five or six years.

There are very attractive varieties of culinary sage with purple leaves (*S. officinalis* 'Purpurascens'), variegated gold leaves (*S. officinalis* 'Icterina'), and pink, white and grey-green leaves (*S. officinalis* 'Tricolor'). The latter can be short-lived. The best variety for cooking and medicinal use is the English broad-leaved sage, which does not flower.

Yellow and white

Poached Egg Plant (Limnanthes douglasii) (hardy annual)

This charming self-seeding annual has yellow and white flowers just like the eponymous poached eggs. It's low-growing and will seed itself around year after year with great abandon. It attracts hoverflies that predate aphids, so it's ideal for companion planting. It flowers from late April until the end of June.

SUMMER

Reds and pinks

Amaranthus caudatus (half-hardy annual)

The wine-red tresses of Love-Lies-Bleeding make a dramatic contrast growing with black kale and the

Amaranthus caudatus – *Love-Lies-Bleeding.*

taller vegetables. It flowers from July until the end of the summer, becoming steadily bigger and producing more flowers. There are pink and white-flowered forms too. They can be dried for winter, either by hanging them upside down, or putting them in a tall jug so that the flowers droop down from their stalks.

Sow the seed in March in a frost-free greenhouse or on a cool window sill. Pot them up individually, then harden them off gradually before planting them out in late May.

Antirrhinum *(half-hardy annual)*
Snapdragons have always had an appeal for children: they love making them 'talk'. They are excellent for picking for the house from July to September, but they would definitely be missed from the garden border. Their upright spikes carry

mostly pink, white and red flowers, but there are yellow varieties and bi-colours too.

Grow them from seed as you would *Amaranthus*. Ensure that the seedlings are tipped out: that is, pinch out the growing tip between finger and thumb to encourage the plant to make side shoots.

Clary sage (Salvia horminum)
(hardy annual)
Clary makes a dramatic impact in any situation. Its pink, blue and mauve flowers are actually 'bracts'. This means that they remain colourful from the moment they begin to flower until the autumn. They are lovely for picking for the house and drying for the winter. Although clary is a member of the sage family, it is not used in cooking or medicinally.

Clary takes up quite a lot of space: about 50cm (20in) in all directions. But there are dwarf forms available that confine themselves to 45cm (18in) tall. Sow the seed under glass in March and plant the seedlings out in May. They should be in flower from July to September.

Cosmos (half-hardy annual)
The annual cosmos is quite different from the 'Chocolate Cosmos' which belongs to the dahlia family. Annual cosmos is spectacular grown in drifts of either mixed pinks and whites, or a single colour. Its big, wide open flowers are attractive to pollinating bees and butterflies and can be picked to bring indoors.

Sow the seed and raise the seedlings as you would *Amaranthus*. Nip out the growing tips and plant them out in May. They will flower from July until the frosts.

Gladiolus (bulb)
Old-fashioned 'glads', with their strong colours and single stems, rarely find a comfortable position in a modern garden, but grown in the ornamental vegetable garden their glorious colours can be indulged. Most gladioli are shades of red and pink, but there are sophisticated lime greens and dark purples that are becoming increasingly fashionable to cut for the house.

They are half-hardy corms that should be planted out only after all danger of frost has passed. If a few are started in pots in the greenhouse they will come into flower earlier. And if others are planted later they will provide a succession of flowers throughout the late summer. Plant them on a layer of sharp sand or grit at twice their own depth in a sunny, well-drained position. In the autumn lift the corms, cut off the fan of leaves and dry them out through the winter under the greenhouse benching or in a frost-free shed or garage.

Hollyhock (Alcea rosea)
(hardy perennial/biennial)
Tall hollyhock spires rising above rows of cabbages and carrots are among the most nostalgic of plants. They conjure up images of thatched cottages and Peter Rabbit. They seem just right for an informal ornamental vegetable garden, although they are grown purely for decoration. The flowers are predominantly pink and pastels, with the exception

A lime-green gladiolus flowers among a drift of white cosmos.

of the 'black' hollyhock. These purple satin flowers are sumptuous with oranges and reds, or add a low note to the pastel pinks and mauves.

They are tall: 180cm (71in). They tend to develop rust, especially if they are grown on as perennials, and they eventually succumb to high winds. But hollyhocks can be used as a biennial to flower just once and then be pulled out. Sow these between April and June and transplant them to their flowering positions in late summer. There are some seed varieties that claim to produce dwarf plants that will flower within the year they are sown. These should be sown directly in the position where they are to flower in early May.

Musk mallow (Malva moschata) (hardy perennial)

The sugar-pink flowers of musk mallows are very ornamental growing among lettuces and other ephemera that are planted around them as the seasons come and go. Their young shoots are delicious added to salads and if the plant is cut back in summer, a second crop will often be produced.

Sow in trays in spring. The seed will germinate better if you first gently rub it between two sheets of fine sandpaper to damage the hard coat. Pot up the seedlings and plant them out in their flowering positions in the summer. They will begin flowering the following summer.

Scented-leaf pelargoniums (Pelargonium species) (tender perennial)

What could be more delightful than placing a few pots of scented-leaf pelargoniums next to your seat in summer? Brush their leaves with your hand and they will release the scent of rose, peppermint or musk. Many have large, usually pink and red, flowers. Others are prettily variegated.

Buy them as young plants in early summer and pot them up. Cuttings are easy to root in August and September and should be kept somewhere frost-free during the winter. The mother plant can then be composted: large plants can host greenfly and other pests in a frost-free greenhouse. Or put mother on the bathroom window sill where you will brush her leaves every time you close the curtains and so release the perfume. Cut her down in spring to an outward-facing bud or shoot; then pot her on

or feed her with an organic liquid fertilizer; and finally put her outdoors again at the end of May. She'll love it.

Sweet peas (hardy annual)

These are a beautiful addition to any ornamental vegetable garden. They could be grown up their own wigwams, or they could consort with the runner beans. These days, there is an enormous range in the pink, red, white and mauve colour schemes. Many seed companies offer a range of varieties with differing amounts of scent. They are all easy to grow and it's possible to have sweet peas in flower from May until August if you sow them at different times of year. Keep picking the flowers to prevent them from setting seed: once a plant has achieved motherhood it stops flowering.

Sweet pea 'Matucana'.

You can start sowing in October, although early November is ideal. If the seed has a hard black coat, soak it overnight first; this will help it to germinate more quickly. Sow two or three seeds to a 7cm (2¾in) pot filled with commercial compost. The pots can be kept in a cold frame during the winter, but watch out for mice. When the seedlings have produced three pairs of true leaves, pinch out the tips. Harden the pots off and plant them out in April in ground that has been improved with plenty of organic matter. These should flower in late May. Another batch of seed can be sown in the same way or directly into the ground during April and May. These should flower from June to August. When sweet peas have finished flowering they quickly shrivel and brown, so it might be advisable to grow the batches in separate positions so that the dying foliage of the early sweet peas does not spoil the later ones.

Blues and mauves

*Borage (*Borago officinalis*)*
(self-seeding hardy annual)
The bright, true-blue flowers of borage are a constant and flattering partner to any of the yellow and orange flowers and vegetables you might grow. They attract bees and hoverflies. The leaves and stems have a cucumber flavour, but can be a bit too hairy to be palatable. The flowers are also cucumber-flavoured: the classic addition to a glass of summer Pimm's. They also decorate salads prettily. In all, they are a must in an ornamental vegetable garden.

Borage grows in almost any soil, whether it is rich and fertile, or poor and sandy. It's quite a tall plant, 60–100cm (24–34in), which can collapse all over its neighbours, so make sure it can do no harm by placing it around taller vegetables or wigwams of runner beans. There is a sparkling white-flowered form too, which stays true from seed if it is grown away from its naturally blue brother.

Sow the seeds directly where you want them to flower: they have fleshy stems that do not transplant well. Once they have been introduced, you will never be without them. Nor will you want to be.

Blue borage.

Chicory flowers.

Chicory *(Cichorum intybus)*
(hardy perennial)

This wild form of the domesticated vegetable bears startling blue flowers that open in the morning and are gone by midday. It's a big, untidy plant that would need staking initially: 120cm (47in). Position it carefully.

Wild chicory is easy to grow from seed sown in April, potted up and planted out either in the autumn, or potted on and kept over the winter in a cold frame or greenhouse. Plant it out the following April.

Lavender *(Lavandula angustifolia)*
(hardy sub-shrub)

This beautiful, scented plant makes a good edging for a formal parterre. There are dwarf forms that would be more suitable than the rather large, rangy, traditional lavenders.

Lavender has been grown for centuries to perfume 'laundered' clothes. (The words have the same Latin root.) The flowers were also tied in bunches and placed in wardrobes to guard against moths eating clothes. Modern cooks are re-discovering their culinary virtues, which were once familiar to the Elizabethans: try a few sprigs to flavour home-made vanilla ice cream.

Lavenders are another Roman introduction, so they too prefer a poor soil. Clip them over lightly in spring and then again to remove the dead flowers in August. Try not to cut back into the wood: they often fail to regenerate.

Lavenders are typically rather short-lived. Take heeled cuttings from the side shoots in May or June when they are about 10cm (4 in). Pot them up when they are rooted, keeping them in a cold frame over the winter. They can be planted out in spring.

This ubiquitous herb of the Mediterranean region is quite at home in the UK, especially in the warmer counties. In late summer it produces billows of mauve-pink flowers that are gate-crashed by every bee in the garden.

Marjoram – pot *(hardy perennial)*

The grey-leaved marjoram is less hardy here, as is its relative, oregano. But there are many different forms of this essential herb, most of which also have mauve bee-flowers.

Pot marjoram makes an overwintering mat of tight, dark green leaves and flowers that extend to about 45cm (18in) in height. They would be happiest at the edge of the beds, gently overspilling on to the path.

Young plants are usually available in spring if you only need a few, or they can be easily grown from seed. Sow the seed in trays in April and May; pot two or three seedlings to a 7cm (2¾in) pot, then keep them in a cold frame or greenhouse for the winter. Plant them out in late spring.

Phacelia tanacetifolia *(hardy annual)*

Not only is *Phacelia* used as a green manure (*see* Chapter 10), but it's highly decorative and very attractive to bees. It bears fat spikes of lavender-mauve flowers about 30cm (12in) tall.

Sow the seed directly where it is to flower in the months of March and April. It will often self-seed the following season.

Statice *(Limonium) and sea lavender (half-hardy annual)*

The cultivated forms of statice are invaluable for drying and their flowers add soft colour to the

Statice.

garden. Selected seed mixes are available in individual shades of apricot, blue, pink and so on. Hang bunches up in a cool, dark, airy place when the flowers are just beginning to open.

Limonium latifolia, or sea lavender, is the wild form, with clouds of tiny lavender flowers on wiry stems. It is possibly even prettier in the garden and dried arrangements than its cultivated cousin. This grows to a height of about 60cm (24in).

Sow the seed in a bit of warmth in March; prick out the seedlings when they are large enough to handle; and plant them out after the frosts are over at the end of May. They flower from July to September at a height of about 45–60cm (18–24in). Sea lavender prefers a well-drained, sunny site.

Thyme (Thymus officinalis)
(hardy perennial)

Thyme is one of the prettiest herbs in the horticultural canon and one of the most varied. The leaves can be variegated or golden; the flowers pink, mauve or white; and the flavour differs widely among the varieties. The classic medicinal and culinary plant, *Thymus officinalis*, is small and twiggy, with mauve flowers in midsummer that are

Verbena bonariensis.

invariably swarming with bees on a sunny day. Thyme needs well-drained soil and lots of sun. It would be ideal to grow at the edge of a bed near, but not next to, marjoram, which is bossier. Or it would behave well and look most attractive in small terracotta pots.

Named forms of thyme can be bought in spring, but *Thymus officinalis* can be raised from seed. Sow in April and May; prick out the seedlings when they are large enough to handle. Then pot them up in 7cm (2¾in) pots in July and August and overwinter them in a cold frame or greenhouse. They can be planted out in spring.

Verbena bonariensis (short-lived hardy perennial)

This tall, transparent flower seems to have become ubiquitous and essential in all modern gardens. It's equally at home growing among grasses and other late-flowering perennials as it is powering up through the late summer vegetables.

Its mauve-purple flowers have a tiny carmine eye that gives them a twinkle and an uncanny knack of looking right in any colour scheme, but they work especially well with the hot reds and oranges of late summer. Bees and butterflies find it as irresistible as twenty-first-century gardeners do.

Sow the seed in trays in early spring under glass. Pot the seedlings up into 7cm (2¾in) pots in April to May and they will be ready to plant out in the summer. *V. bonariensis* is happy to seed itself in poor soils in full sun, so you may well find it prefers your path to the rich soil of the vegetable beds.

Yellows and oranges

Dahlias – (tender tuberous perennials)

Dahlias are not, of course, just yellow and orange: they produce emphatic blooms in a huge colour range. But those colours are saturated and strong and they mostly fit in well with other fiery flowers. They are eminently suited to growing in an ornamental vegetable garden where they can be staked, primped and preened, before eventually being picked for the house.

Dahlias.

Helichrysum.

Dahlias grow best in well-manured ground. Plant out the tubers or young plants after the frosts are over and stake them. Keep the flowers either picked or dead-headed to keep them coming, and feed the plant with tomato fertilizer weekly. Lift the tubers after the first frost in the autumn has felled the top-growth and clean off the soil. Lay the tubers in dry peat or compost in boxes in a garage or frost-free garden shed. Keep them just slightly damp until March, when they can be brought into a light, frost-free greenhouse and started into growth again.

Helichrysum *(straw flowers)*
(half-hardy annual)
The crisp orange, red and gold flowers make a vibrant splash in the sun. Their shining petals have the texture of straw. They look best growing in their own dedicated patch rather than in close proximity to rows of cabbages and beans. And they flower better too in poorer soil and without too much crowding.

Pick the heads just before they open fully, then hang them in bunches upside down in a cool, airy and dark place such as the garage or the corner of the garden shed. Sow them in a warm place in spring. Prick them out and pot them up, keeping them under frost-free glass. Plant them out towards the end of May when all danger of frost is past.

Marigolds – French *(*Tagetes*)*
(half-hardy annual)

Dwarf French marigolds bring more colour to the garden from late June onwards. Many varieties are multi-coloured blood red, orange and yellow. Importantly, they are one of the most attractive hosts for hoverflies (*see* Chapter 10). However, in order to synchronize their flowering with that of runner beans and other pestered crops, it may be wise to sow them somewhere warm in February. Prick them out and pot them up, keeping them frost-free. Plant them out when all danger of frost is past in late May. By then, they should be almost in flower and ready to stand guard alongside the young beans.

*Pot marigolds (*Calendula*).*

Marigolds – pot *(*Calendula*)*
(hardy annual)

The uncompromising orange of pot marigolds is almost incandescent. The variety 'Touch of Red' has fiery red undersides and tips to the flowers that seem to fan the flames. Pot marigolds are glorious growing with blue borage or the dark purple *Lavandula* 'Hidcote'. And they positively vibrate alongside red cabbages, beetroot and purple kale. Their orange petals have a delicious tang in salads and they are gorgeous in a little brown jug on the garden table.

They should not, however, be confused with *Tagetes*, the French marigolds, which host hoverflies. On the contrary, pot marigolds do harbour blackfly. Plant them well away from beans and anything else that is susceptible to blackfly.

Sow them where they are to flower in April in a sunny place. If they are happy they will seed themselves around and among the vegetables.

Nasturtium

Perhaps not ideal plants for a vegetable garden, nasturtiums somehow win through on their looks alone. Their vivacious red, orange and yellow horned flowers clamber over the beds and spill on to the paths with an engaging enthusiasm in late summer. But they do attract blackfly, and even cabbage white caterpillars will find them palatable.

French marigolds growing with white cosmos.

Nasturtium.

There is an argument for nasturtiums 'distracting' their attentions away from your other vegetable crops, but it could equally be said to help increase the populations of such destructive pests.

Nevertheless, if you succumb to their *joie de vivre* the seed is usually sown where it is to flower in April, or it can be started off in pots in a cold greenhouse in March to flower a month earlier in about June.

Rudbeckia fulgida *'Goldsturm'*
(hardy perennial)

The old fashioned 'black-eyed Suzy' is still one of the most popular and bright flowers in late summer. Its dark brown central boss of stamens is surrounded by sunny yellow daisy petals. It flowers from midsummer until the first frosts of winter, then dies back to a resting crown of rough green

Rudbeckia fulgida *'Goldsturm'*.

Sunflower seed head.

leaves. Bees and butterflies home in on a patch of them from all parts of the garden.

They are often available to buy as young plants from nurseries and garden centres in spring, or you could start them off from seed. Sow in April and pot up as many seedlings as you might need. Plant them out where they are to flower in late summer, nipping out any premature buds. They will flower the following year.

Sunflower (hardy annual)

Sunflowers have recently become very popular as late summer cut flowers, but if you leave their wonderful big heads until the autumn the seeds will ripen. And if you get in first before the birds, the seeds can be collected and dried and are delicious mixed with breakfast cereal, or roasted like peanuts.

Nowadays, there are some lovely autumnal colours to choose from: browns and tans, gold and primrose, as well as striped and double flowers. The tall ones produce just one flowering spike, but many of the newer varieties can be tipped out and will then branch to give a continuity of somewhat smaller flowers.

The French name for sunflower is *tournesol*, because the flowers turn to face the sun as it appears to cross the sky every day. Be sure to have done the homework before you show them to children!

Sow two seeds to a 7cm (2¾in) pot, discarding the weaker at true-leaf stage. Pot them on, harden them off and plant them out in May. Even the lower-branching ones will need staking from the start. The giants may need extra support.

Green-leaved herbs

Basil (half-hardy annual)

The soft green leaves of sweet basil are best grown in a shallow terracotta pot and placed somewhere sunny. There is also a lovely variety with purple-red leaves for contrast. And there are many different forms of basil that are suitable for different styles of cooking, such as Neapolitan and Genovese basils for Italian dishes; Thai basil that has dark green leaves and deep purple flowers on a somewhat taller plant; lemon basil and very many other distinctively flavoured forms.

They all need very sharp drainage and full sun. When planted out into the beds they run the risk of rotting off, or of making a midnight feast for an insomniac slug.

Sow the seed very thinly directly into shallow pots in late April. Maintain a temperature of about 18°C (64°F) for germination: a heated propagator works well. Thin the seedlings carefully so that there is space for the passage of air; basil suffers badly from damping off. Gradually lower the temperature and harden off the seedlings under frost-free protection. The pots can be placed outdoors from the beginning of June when all danger of frost is past.

Coriander (half-hardy annual)

The soft foliage of coriander changes as it matures into feathery leaves, which eventually produce an umbel of small yellow flowers. Cut the young leaves regularly while they are still the shape of flat-leaved parsley. The plants will carry on producing leaves until eventually they run to flower and seed. Both the leaves and the seeds are an essential ingredient of Indian food and their distinctive flavour can be added to very many other dishes.

Treat the seed like basil. Coriander can be grown in a large, shallow pot, or sow it directly in a sunny position where it is to grow. Like basil, coriander dislikes being transplanted. Cover the seedlings and

A bed of fennel.

young plants with a cloche until the end of May in order to protect them from the frost and give them a warm start.

Dill (hardy annual)

There is little to compare with the flavour of dill. Its pretty feathery foliage looks like fennel, but the plant is shorter at about 90cm (35in). It produces attractive umbels of yellow flowers in June and July, sets seed and dies. Pinch out the growing tip to delay flowering. Dill goes well with most fish dishes, especially salmon, while the leaves and flowers are a common ingredient in pickles and as a flavouring in oil and vinegar.

Sow a patch of dill where it is to flower. Thin the seedlings to leave them about 5–8cm (2–3in) apart in late April or early March.

Fennel (hardy perennial)

The tall feathery foliage of fennel is lovely growing among the vegetables. By August it produces umbels of yellow flowers at about 2m (79in) that gradually set seed. It spends the winter as an underground tap root that is very difficult to dig out, so sow or plant it where it is to remain and be vigilant with its seedlings.

Bronze fennel has the same aniseed flavour as the green-leaved form, but in spring and early summer its plumes of shining brown leaves are very decorative.

Sow the seed where it is to flower in April and thin the seedlings down to two or three per square metre (1.2sq yd). If you don't want self-sown volunteers, cut off the seed head before it goes brown and ripens.

Feverfew (hardy perennial)

The open-eyed daisies of feverfew are very pretty among low-growing vegetables. The golden-leaved form is even more attractive. It flowers at about 50–60cm (20–24in) and makes a tidy mound all summer. Feverfew is a proven preventative for some forms of migraine. Those who find it effective roll up a bitter-tasting leaf like a pill and swallow it with water. But it does attract blackfly, so keep the plants away from the beans.

Feverfew is easy to grow from seed sown in April and May. Pot up the seedlings and plant them out

in the summer. At this stage slugs and snails, which are not known to suffer from migraines, find the leaves irresistible. Alternatively, young plants are usually available to be planted out, ideally in June. Choose a sunny spot with rich but draining soil. Allow at least 30cm (12in) between the plants. You may well find there are some self-sown seedlings the following spring.

Mint (hardy perennial)

Many forms of mint produce beautiful lavender flowers like little buddleias. Apple mint has very attractive cream and grey-green leaves. There are many different forms of mint to choose from, all of which are highly invasive if let loose anywhere, especially in the rich soil of your vegetable beds. But they are well worth planting in a pot for their flowers and delicious leaves.

Buy young plants in spring and pot them up into a decorative container. Put the container in a saucer or the roots could escape through the drainage hole and launch an invasion into the beds.

After two or three years the container will have become quite congested, so tip out the plant and cut it in half with a spade. Overcrowded mint is susceptible to rust. Replace the better half in the pot with fresh commercial compost. Unless you want to pot up the other half, put it in the bin, not on the compost heap.

Parsley (biennial)

The lovely curly leaves of traditional parsley make a good edging for vegetable beds. As biennials, the plants will only occupy the space for a year and a half, so you could change the edging the following summer. Alternatively, a few plants would look good in a large pot ready to be cut for the kitchen. If you bring the pots indoors they will provide leaves throughout the winter too. In France, plain-leaved parsley is more popular than it is over here. The French maintain it has a better flavour than the curled varieties. The leaves resemble coriander and when cut it's hard to work out the difference without tasting them.

Parsley is notoriously reluctant to germinate. The seed needs to be started off in late March with some bottom heat in a propagator, or sown later at the end of April under glass. If it's sown directly in April

and May, it can take up to six weeks to germinate. Prick out the seedlings when they are large enough to handle and plant them out in May, leaving about 15cm (6in) between the plants. They will be ready to harvest from late June until late autumn. In the spring they can be cut for a few weeks before they run to flower.

Sorrel – buckler-leaved (hardy perennial)

The soft green leaves are the shape of a shield, hence its common name. They make pale mounds about 30cm (12in) high, ideally at the edge of the beds. However, these fleshy mounds make excellent hiding places for fat, fleshy slugs, so check them over regularly. The flavour of sorrel is worth all the problems, however. It has a sharp lemony tang to the leaves.

Grow it from seed sown in spring and planted out in late summer, or buy one or two young plants from a specialist nursery.

Tarragon – French (tender perennial)

This makes a low plant resembling small rosemary, but French tarragon has no flowers. Its unique flavour is imparted during cooking to chicken and fish dishes. Russian tarragon looks very similar, but its flavour is different and inferior to the French form. Grow French tarragon in a pot for the summer alongside the basil and coriander and protect it during the winter out of the frost.

The seed that is offered is always that of Russian tarragon; French tarragon can only be propagated from cuttings. Take 10cm (4in) shoots in early summer, then root them in a mix of horticultural grit and sterilized loam, or all-purpose compost. They root easily and quickly and can be potted up for use by midsummer.

CHAPTER 10

Organic gardening

Throughout this book it has not been assumed that vegetables should be grown organically. Where appropriate, the conventional, non-organic method of pest and disease control, soil preparation and treatment and use of fertilizers has been indicated. But in today's climate of concern about the health of the planet and we who live on it, growing edible crops organically finds much popular support.

For many vegetable growers the appeal of growing food for the family without recourse to chemicals is the main reason for all the work involved. It may be a question of degree, however. For many gardeners, it's the knowledge that what is eaten does not contain any trace of chemical pesticide that's important. For some, it's the case that their garden is also friendly to all living creatures: the birds, bees, insects and wildlife.

For others, treating the soil, the plants and the wildlife with care and consideration is the means to a better life. Each natural element is a part of the whole, including ourselves. The only way to build up a natural balance is by caring for the soil and the living organisms in and on it. In this way, problems such as pests and diseases are kept to a minimum. Natural predators will rise in population in proportion to their prey. Soil that is enriched with organic matter will naturally be high in microbes, which will in turn support the health and strong growth of crops.

Although most gardeners would agree with these aims, there has never been an exact definition of the word 'organic'. We all think we know what it means. But all living things are made up of organic chemicals and chemically the term refers

Leeks, alfalfa and French marigolds.

only to carbon. It would be more accurate to call it 'gardening with nature' or 'environmental/eco-friendly gardening'. That would imply the idea of working with nature instead of against it, which is what most 'organic' gardeners are aiming to achieve. But the term has emerged and, accurate or not, 'organic' gardening is here to stay.

Increasingly, as more horticultural chemicals are being withdrawn from the amateur market every year, today's gardeners have to use far more organic methods than their grandfathers. Until long after the Second World War tomatoes were routinely sprayed with nicotine, and during Victorian times much use was made of 'tobacco water', paraffin, train oil and soot. Amazingly, nineteenth-century gardening books advised that a kitten be tied with a long string to a wire lined along a row of newly sown vegetables to scare off the birds: organic maybe, but hardly benign.

However, organic gardening is not an exact science. Some would argue that much is not scientific at all. It's only recently that more objective research is being carried out on some of these methods to verify hearsay evidence. Some methods have proven to work well, while others work to a more limited extent, but are an improvement on doing nothing. And many do not work at all, they just sound good. Over the past few years the Internet has been providing a forum for discussion and to exchange first-hand experience of different organic methods and remedies. There's everything there, from scientific research papers to blogs by gardening enthusiasts.

Many of the methods outlined in this chapter are those used in some of the gardens that are examined and illustrated throughout the book. The extent to which a method does or does not work is outlined. And sometimes the failure to use the organic method provides evidence that it works: the exception proving the rule.

STARTING WITH THE SOIL

Garden compost

Incorporating organic matter into the soil at the right time is one of the most important factors in keeping the ground in good heart. By this, it is meant that the soil can support healthy growth that will give your vegetables the strength to resist affliction. Farmyard manure that has been rotted down for at least a year is ideal, but in addition to manure, or in its place, you could use home-made garden compost.

By putting vegetable matter on to the compost heap you will be returning the nutrients in that matter to the soil when the compost is added prior to planting. Soil-borne organisms break down the matter, fixing the nitrogen and leaving nutrients available for the plants to absorb. In time, the texture of the compost will be like Christmas cake: rich, crumbly and slightly fibrous. Added to the soil, organic matter will break up the clay particles, as well as acting as a sponge. When the sponge is full of moisture and cannot hold any more, the excess will run away. Thus the soil will never become wet and boggy.

There is plenty of literature on making compost and compost heaps. Almost every gardener swears by his or her own method, but there are some basics and some golden rules.

- If there is space, the ideal is three compost heaps: one to fill; one to rot down; and one to use. But if you turn the resting heap with a fork regularly it will rot down more quickly and two heaps would be sufficient. Every time you turn it, add some accelerator. You can buy it in boxes in the form of 'urea', or you can make your own: recycle those cups of tea. (It's easier for the chaps!)

- Many gardeners cover the heap with a piece of old carpet to increase the heat and thereby speed up the decomposition. As organic matter decays, the activity of the micro-organisms causes heat to build up. Think of those steaming heaps of fresh manure. The heap should be at least 1m (39in) square. Any smaller and it will not heat up very well, so decomposition will be slower. Furthermore it could freeze in cold weather, killing the busy bacteria, or dry out in the summer with the same effect.

- Air is important to those bacteria and organisms too. If there is no oxygen during decomposition it becomes anaerobic, the organisms die and the result is a slimy, foul-smelling mess. So do not

---

WHAT TO COMPOST AND WHAT NOT TO COMPOST

Do compost:

- green vegetable matter from the garden
- uncooked vegetable waste from the kitchen
- annual weeds that are not seeding
- the tops of perennial weeds without their roots or seeds (nettles and comfrey are especially valuable)
- grass clippings mixed with any of the above
- fallen leaves
- torn up newspapers and envelopes
- green stems of woody plants that have been chopped up
- soiled straw waste from pets or stables (except dog and cat litter)
- top growth from green manures (*see* below).

Never compost:

- perennial weeds such as docks, bindweed, ground elder and so on; the compost heap may not be hot enough to destroy the pernicious roots
- weeds that are in flower or seeding; again, the heap has to be really hot to destroy seeds
- meat and fish scraps, bones or oil, as these attract rats and vermin to the heap
- woody and thorny prunings: they can take years to break down
- ash from coal or coke, although wood ash is fine in moderation: it's full of potassium
- diseased plants or vegetables, including blighted tomatoes
- dog and cat excrement (although rabbit, hamster and guinea pig droppings are okay)
- soiled disposable nappies; these are unhygienic and contain plastic, which takes centuries to break down
- glossy magazines
- plastic.

---

pile in mounds of grass clippings, mix them up with the kitchen green waste; and if you add newspapers, tear them up first so that they are not piled up in thick wodges.

- Add accelerator at 30cm (12in) intervals to start off the process while you are still filling up the heap. Top off the heap with a layer of animal manure if possible.

Green manure

The term 'green manure' can seem a little confusing. It is shorthand for certain crops that are grown entirely for the purpose of digging them into the soil in order to increase its fertility and improve the structure. It's an old idea that is finding increasing favour with modern organic and conventional gardeners.

Besides returning nutrients to the soil, green manure adds lots of fibre to both heavy clay soils to break them up and to light sandy soils to help with moisture retention. Some of the plants used are leguminous: they have nitrogen-fixing nodules on their roots. That is, they fix nitrogen from the atmosphere to add to the nitrogen already present.

A green manure is sown in an area vacated by a previous crop, often at the end of the summer and into the autumn. This draws up and uses the remaining nutrients in the soil. Then when this plant is turned into the soil, those nutrients contained in the leaves and stems are returned to become available again to the next crop, thereby avoiding the unused nutrients in the soil being washed away with the winter rains.

When it is turned into the soil, it's important to allow at least a week or two for the green manure to break down, or there will be a deficiency of nitrogen in the soil. Cut up the stems and leaves of larger-growing green manures. Use a strimmer or a rotary mower if practical. The plants can then be turned into the soil at a fairly shallow depth: 15cm (6in) is sufficient.

When crop seed is sown in the area it will take a few weeks to germinate and put down roots. In the meantime, the green manure below ground is continuing to break down. Ideally, therefore, wait a little longer than a couple of weeks before planting out pot-raised vegetables and plugs, or use a quick-fix fertilizer that is high in nitrogen to get the young plants growing while the green manure continues to break down. This is also advisable if the green-manure plants have become a little woody.

If necessary, the green manure can be turned into the soil when it is at the seedling stage. This practice is of most benefit between the lines of slower growing vegetables also at the seedling stage. The green manure effectively soaks up the excess nutrients in the soil and then returns them later as and when the crop grows bigger.

An additional way of using green manures is to harvest them and add them to the compost heap. This is especially useful for leguminous plants and those that occupy the ground for a whole season.

It's inadvisable to allow the green manure to flower and run to seed. Not only does that mean you will have its progeny popping up everywhere, but the seedlings may be robbing the soil of nutrients that are there for the crop. In theory, also, the plants as they flower make different plant chemicals that may not be useful to the crop.

When choosing a green manure for a specific plot take account of what type of plant it is and

Phacelia and Hungarian rye sown as a green manure in vacant soil.

whether it is related to the vegetables you are growing. For example mustard belongs to the brassicas; and nitrogen-fixing members of the pea family, the legumes, should not be planted prior to sowing root vegetables. The green manure should form part of the crop rotation.

SPECIES USED FOR GREEN MANURE

- Red clover has nitrogen-fixing nodules on its extensive root system as it's a member of the pea family. It should ideally be sown in spring and grown as part of a crop rotation to occupy a bed for an entire season. It improves the texture of the soil and its fertility. Clovers can also be cut over and the trimmings added to the compost heap.
- Phacelia is attractive enough to grow for its flowers alone, but if it's being grown as a green manure it should be sown in early September and dug in the following spring before it can run to flower. Leave the ground for at least two weeks before sowing the crop. The seed is expensive to buy, but it could be saved from those plants grown for their flowers. It is not nitrogen-fixing.
- Field beans (*Vicia faba*) are sown in autumn to be incorporated before sowing in spring. Their roots contain nitrogen-fixing nodules that will feed leafy vegetables in particular.
- Lupins are nitrogen-fixing legumes and they also add phosphorous to the soil. They prefer more acidic soils and are deep rooting, so they pull up nutrients from lower down. The agricultural species are half-hardy annuals, so sow them in spring and incorporate the plants after two to three months, before they flower.
- Alfalfa, or lucerne, is also deep rooted and can resist drought well, although it does occupy space for a long time and can be left *in situ* for more than a season. It is not nitrogen-fixing, but seed is sometimes sold that has been treated with the bacteria rhizobium that does fix nitrogen. It can be strimmed down periodically to provide plenty of green matter both for the compost heap and when it is dug in.
- Common buckwheat (*Fagopyrum esculentum*) is not related to wheat but is a member of the bean family: a legume. It's best left to occupy a space for an entire summer to improve the soil with its tall and voluminous top growth and extensive root system. Buckwheat is a half-hardy annual so it cannot be sown in autumn to overwinter.
- Mustard (*Sinapsis alba*) is a useful fast-growing green manure which makes lots of top growth that suppresses the weeds and can be dug in within six to eight weeks of sowing. It is, however, a member of the brassica family, so it could host diseases of cabbages such as club root.
- Winter tares (*Vicia villosa*) are hardy annuals. They are a traditional arable crop that was grown on ground left fallow for a year. Tares are best sown from July to September and allowed to occupy vacant ground until the spring. The crop is then dug in during the late spring prior to sowing. It dislikes dry, acid soils, but it fixes nitrogen and makes plenty of top growth to improve the fertility and texture of the soil. It can also be sown between March and May and dug in between the end of May until July.

Common buckwheat.

WEED ERADICATION AND CONTROL

Some weeds are worse than others. Anyone who has been faced with a sea of ground elder or a forest of bindweed will envy their neighbour with only docks and dandelions to deal with. It is very tempting to start digging up the roots. Bindweed has easily identifiable, thick white roots and ground elder has thinner ones. The problem is that they are en route for Australia. It is quite impossible to dig out all the roots and the tiniest piece of root left in the soil will produce a bigger and better plant than its dad. So digging over the patch in winter is a shortcut to making the problem ten times worse.

The organic method of ridding the soil of these weeds is to blanket the entire area for a year to cut out the light, using sheets of black woven matting, coir matting, used woollen carpeting or cardboard. Woven matting is made of plastic and is pretty tough, while also allowing moisture to penetrate through into the soil. Coir matting fulfils the same function, but is easier on the eye. Old woollen carpeting similarly cuts out the light from the weeds. Cardboard laid down thickly works as well in the short term, but by the end of the summer it will have downgraded completely. If the summer is wet and the cardboard rots away too quickly there's a good chance that the bindweed or ground elder will seize the opportunity to grow through.

Whatever material you choose, ensure that the edges are well covered: pernicious perennial weeds have a way of finding an escape route. Uncover the ground in the spring after a year has passed and it should be ready for the next stage.

Less pernicious weeds such as docks, dandelions, couch grass, nettles and creeping buttercups can be dug out successfully with a border fork. Ensure that every last bit of root is removed and don't put them on the compost heap.

Annual weeds such as hairy bittercress, the scourge of every gardener and nurseryman in the country, should be pulled or hoed out before they start to flower. If you can see the flowers some of them will have already seeded. Use the 'stale seedbed technique' to clear the ground in spring of annual weeds (*see* Chapter 5).

Mulching the ground once your vegetables are growing helps to prevent annual weed seedlings from germinating, as well as retaining soil moisture. Local councils are a source of excellent coarse-grade mulches made from green waste. If you use wood chippings, sawdust or shavings, they would need to have been composted for at least a year to degrade, otherwise they might cause nitrogen deficiencies in the soil. There are commercially available coarse-grade tree bark mulches that are attractive and very effective. They tend to leave marauding slugs and snails high and dry too, although bark mulch is not completely effective. Cocoa shells can be used; they are a by-product of the chocolate industry. They are very effective and are less likely to lock up nitrogen than bark or chippings. But you might have an issue with their carbon footprint.

Regular hoeing prevents weeds becoming a time-consuming problem.

ORGANIC FERTILIZERS

Nutrients

Unlike man-made chemical fertilizers, organic fertilizers take time to break down and release their nutrients to the vegetables. So it pays to think and plan ahead.

As we have seen, different plants have different nutrient requirements from the soil. Some of these nutrients, especially nitrogen, are supplied through the use of garden compost, green manures and animal dung. This will have been incorporated into the soil at the appropriate time for each crop. Potash can be added by scattering bonfire ash lightly among fruiting crops such as peas and beans, courgettes and pumpkins.

Liquid feeds

Liquid feeds give a quicker fix over a short time. They should be used to top up plants that are looking deficient in vital nutrients, or to give a quick boost to young plants in spring. They are not an alternative to using slower-acting organic fertilizer.

Gardeners in the past used to collect horse manure off the road, shovel it into a bucket and top it up with water. After a week or two this fragrant liquid was siphoned off and diluted, then sprayed on and around cabbages and lettuces as a liquid nitrogen feed. These days, seaweed extract is perhaps a more popular organic product that provides a range of nutrients and can be applied throughout the season to everything except root crops.

Liquid feeds can be made by steeping nettles or comfrey in buckets of water for a couple of weeks, then diluting one part to fifty to one hundred parts of water and either spraying on to the foliage, or into the soil beneath the appropriate crops. Nettles are high in nitrogen and comfrey is high in potassium. The exact dose is a matter of experiment: err on the side of caution. Phosphorus can be found in fat hen and vetch. It would be worth experimenting with liquid feeds that are made in a similar way to encourage good root growth. It might work on carrots and parsnips.

The faster, stronger and more robustly a crop is growing, the better it can resist the onslaught of insect pests and fungal diseases. And the real secret to healthy plants lies under the ground in the fertility and life of the soil.

Compost tea

Compost tea is becoming increasingly recognized as a valuable addition to the health of garden soil. Scientific research is backing up the hearsay evidence of gardeners who have been using it for years. It works on the soil by increasing the population of microbes that break down the nutrients and make them available to the plants. The finished 'tea' should be applied to the soil in dilution from a watering can. Use one part tea to twenty parts of water. At a greater dilution the tea can be used as a foliar feed, although the sensitivities of different vegetables to the various teas have not as yet been scientifically tested.

Mycorrhizal fungi

Research is increasingly finding that mycorrhizal fungi have a greater part to play in plant health than has ever been suspected. It has long been known that these soil-dwelling fungi grow symbiotically with certain plants. They help their host plant to absorb nutrients and the fungal mats store water. It has been found that chemical fertilizers can damage the fungi and therefore the health of the plant is diminished. It is possible to buy the spores of these mycorrhizal fungi in a packet, sprinkle them on the ground and rake them in around vegetables, flowers and shrubs. The results are encouraging.

PEST AND DISEASE CONTROL

There are one or two actions that anyone can take to deter pests and diseases in the vegetable garden: keeping everything clean, wiping down spades and forks, and clearing away dead leaves from the beds all help to prevent problems. Fungal diseases can easily be transmitted on garden tools, and leaf litter hides slugs and snails.

Staying vigilant for weeds that host pests and diseases over the winter will reduce their onslaught in the spring, while hoeing regularly between the

---

MAKING COMPOST TEA

- Half-fill a lidded water butt.

- Put comfrey or nettles that have been composted for three months in a netting bag with a drawstring top and tie it to the lid. There should be 700g to every 10ltr of water.

- Top up the water to three-quarters full in the butt.

- Add a little unsulphured molasses to the mixture.

- Let it stand for four weeks. (It will become very smelly indeed!)

- Strain the liquid tea before you use it.

The netting bag of comfrey is attached to the underside of the lid of a water butt so that it is immersed like a teabag in the water.

---

vegetable plants prevents annual weeds from getting a foothold.

Timing the sowing of vulnerable crops such as carrots and onions to miss the peak time for attack by their predators also works well. All these tricks amount to good husbandry.

One of the most enjoyable methods of pest control is to provide habitat and winter rations for the birds. By providing nest boxes, planting hedges and leaving corners of the garden untidied so that insect life can proliferate, you will encourage more birds to take up residence in your garden. Feeding them between October and May will help them to raise larger families and increase the bird population, especially tits. These pretty little acrobats of the bird world can then spend the summer upside-down among the peas and cabbages, pecking off the aphids and caterpillars. They are pretty good with roses, too.

Resistant seed strains

Over the past few years, vegetable breeders have worked to develop strains of carrots, leeks, onions and very many other popular vegetables that are resistant to their specific major pests and diseases. Although these varieties are not immune, their endemic resistance allied to other organic controls means that almost 100 per cent of the crop is clean. Modern resistant varieties are listed wherever possible under each vegetable in Chapter 8.

Companion planting

The idea of companion planting takes several different forms; some are more successful than others. Understanding the life cycle and *modus operandi* of each pest is helpful when it comes to combating and preventing its ill intentions.

Chives edge the carrot border.

French marigolds are grown beneath the broad beans.

Carrot root flies are attracted to their prey by scent. The most vulnerable time is when the carrots are being thinned and release their attractive carroty smell. If a barrier of chives is planted along the edge of the raised bed not only do they interrupt the low flight path of the carrot root fly, but when the surrounding chives are brushed as the carrots are being pulled, they release a stronger smell. And if a resistant variety of carrot is planted the result is total success.

French marigolds (*Tagetes*) are attractive to the larvae of one of nature's best allies, the hoverfly. From their little orange homes they develop into

Nasturtium leaves eaten by cabbage white caterpillars.

the adult form and fly off to find their prey: greenfly and blackfly. Their appetites are huge. *Tagetes* are well worth raising and planting near runner beans, broad beans and peas in particular, so that when the hoverfly larvae hatch the adults have only a short hop to their nearest take-away.

Tagetes minuta is also reputed to help in the control of eelworms and weeds, but it's best used in combination with other methods. It has not been found effective enough to replace other controls.

Less well proven is the idea of attracting pests to another location with decoy plants that draw them away from the vegetables. Nasturtiums not only attract blackfly, but the cabbage white caterpillars have a taste for them too. Whether the nasturtiums distract the butterflies away from the cabbage, or whether they provide additional food for the caterpillars and thereby increase the population of their butterflies, is arguable – and not proven, although hearsay favours the distraction argument.

Organic slug and snail deterrents

Slugs and snails are Public Enemy Number One to most gardeners, organic or not, and there are plenty of alternative suggestions for protecting those vulnerable vegetables, most of which are partially successful. There are quite a few deterrents. 'Slug pubs' are traps filled with beer or some other sweet liquid that attracts slugs and snails to a watery death. Copper strips work well around the rim of pots providing they are renewed every season. Coarsely ground oyster shells sprinkled around the plants also act a barrier. They are available from agricultural merchants for use in chicken feed. They work demonstrably well, as can be seen in the comparison photographs (*see* page 169).

Biological controls within the greenhouse

A greenhouse provides not just tomatoes and aubergines with the ideal habitat, it is also perfect for raising hordes of aphids, whitefly and red spider mites. And these pests have no natural enemies under glass: no birds, no hoverflies and few ladybirds.

Over the past twenty years research has come up with an effective and organic answer: natural predators. These are available through garden centres or on-line. Order them when you are entirely sure that your plants have been infested: the pest has to be there first, or the predators will starve.

When the package arrives open it in the greenhouse immediately and, following the instructions carefully, disperse the predators throughout the growing area. Keep the windows and door closed as much as possible, especially at first, so that the predators can hatch, locate their prey and tuck in.

Each predator is specific to a certain pest:

- *Encarsia formosa* is supplied on cards that should be hung underneath the leaves of plants infected with whitefly. It's a small parasitic wasp that lays its eggs inside the larvae. Whitefly larvae go through many stages of development and some biological control companies repeat the supply

A young courgette with no evidence of slug damage.

A neighbouring young cabbage damaged by slugs: the oyster shells had run out just there.

every two weeks over a six-week period so that every last hatching is prevented.
- *Phytoseiulus persimilis* is a predatory mite that attacks red spider mites (RSM). The nymphs and adults feed voraciously on the RSM and reduce the population quickly. They are effective over a wide temperature range from 4–28°C (39–82°F) and can be used outdoors if necessary.
- Ladybirds can also be bought in; their larvae and adults feed on aphids and thrips.

Other deterrents

Netting crops is not very ornamental, but in many cases it is the most efficient way of preventing attack from pigeons, cabbage white butterflies, rabbits and even deer. Netting does occasionally snare birds, however, and care should be taken to make sure that the edges are firmly bedded down into the soil. Fine horticultural fleece is also very successful in combating winged pests, but perhaps is even less ornamental than netting.

Sowing and Harvesting Calendar

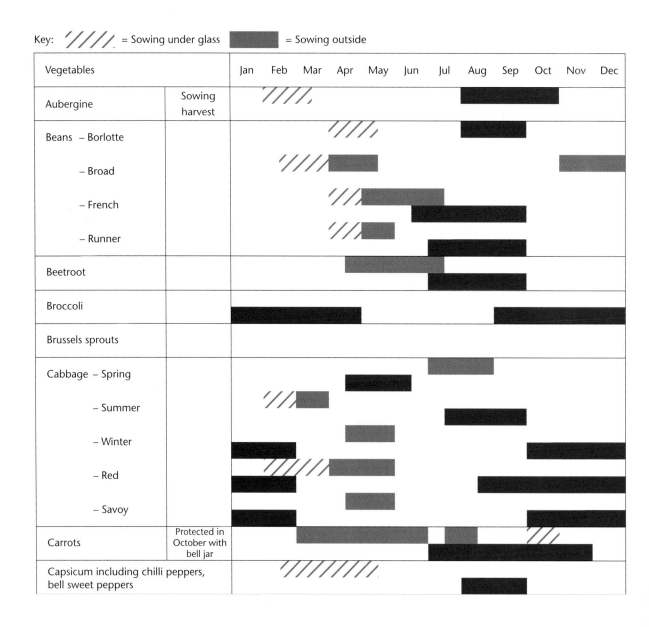

Key: ///// = Sowing under glass   = Sowing outside

Vegetables		Jan	Feb	Mar	Apr	May	Jun	Jul	Aug	Sep	Oct	Nov	Dec
Aubergine	Sowing harvest												
Beans – Borlotte													
– Broad													
– French													
– Runner													
Beetroot													
Broccoli													
Brussels sprouts													
Cabbage – Spring													
– Summer													
– Winter													
– Red													
– Savoy													
Carrots	Protected in October with bell jar												
Capsicum including chilli peppers, bell sweet peppers													

Key: 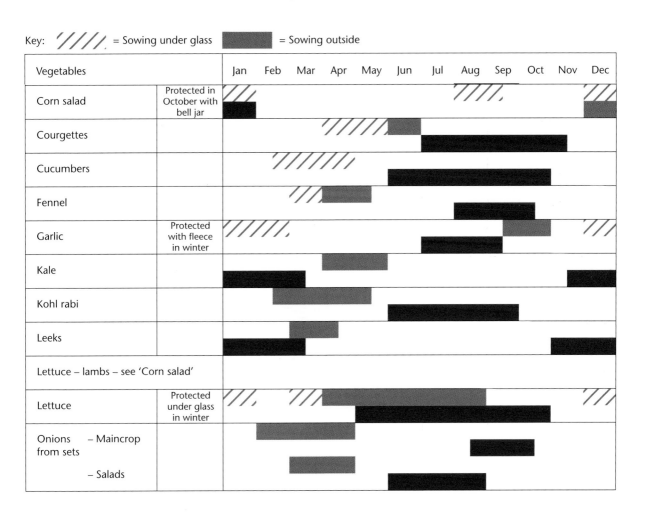 = Sowing under glass   = Sowing outside

Vegetables		Jan	Feb	Mar	Apr	May	Jun	Jul	Aug	Sep	Oct	Nov	Dec
Corn salad	Protected in October with bell jar												
Courgettes													
Cucumbers													
Fennel													
Garlic	Protected with fleece in winter												
Kale													
Kohl rabi													
Leeks													
Lettuce – lambs – see 'Corn salad'													
Lettuce	Protected under glass in winter												
Onions – Maincrop from sets													
– Salads													

		Jan	Feb	Mar	Apr	May	Jun	Jul	Aug	Sep	Oct	Nov	Dec
Onions – Japanese	Sowing / harvest												
Parsnip	Protect under cloches in winter												
Peas – Autumn sown													
– First early													
– Second early													
– Maincrop													
– Management + sugar snap													
- Asparagus													
Potatoes – Early	In pots												
– Main crop	In pots												
Pumpkins + squashes													
Radicchio													
Radish													
Salad rocket													
Salsify													
Shallots													
Spinach – Summer													
– Perpetual													
Sweetcorn													
Swiss chard – see 'Perpetual Spinach'													
Tomatoes – greenhouse													

Glossary

AGM Award of Garden Merit, which is given by the Royal Horticultural Society to exceptionally good vegetables and plants. They are selected from field trials that test for reliability, disease resistance and suitability for most gardens in the UK.

Allium The onion family.

Annual A plant that grows from seed, flowers and sets its own seed within the space of one year. It can only be propagated by seed, not by taking cuttings.

Anthocyanin The red pigment in leaves and plants such as beetroot and ruby chard.

Aphicide A compound, chemical or non-chemical, that is formulated to target blackfly, greenfly and other aphids. It will not affect other insects.

Biennial A plant that grows from seed in its first year to form a rosette or crown. In the second year the flower is produced and seed is set. The plant then dies.

Brassica The cabbage family.

Chlorophyll The green pigment in leaves and stems that is essential for the process of photosynthesis.

Damping off A virulent fungal disease, usually of seedlings, where a patch of mould appears and spreads quickly to infect the entire batch.

Dormant/dormancy A plant or seed that is alive or viable but not actively growing is dormant or in a state of dormancy.

Drill A shallow depression in the soil formed with the corner of the rake ready for seed sowing.

Earthing up Drawing up soil with a rake or mattock to cover the top growth of young potatoes, for example.

Flavin The yellow pigment in leaves and plants such as gold-leaved feverfew.

Germination The process by which a seed starts to grow, sometimes after a period of dormancy.

Hardening off Acclimatizing a plant that has been grown under protection to the higher levels of light and the cooler, fluctuating temperatures outside.

Hardiness A plant's ability to withstand winter temperatures outside in the UK.

Legume The pea family, whose roots have nitrogen-fixing bacteria.

Perennial A plant that endures through the winter and does not die when it sets seed.

pH The name of a logarithmic scale measuring the acidity and alkalinity of a substance.

Photosynthesis The process by which a plant converts carbon dioxide and water in the presence of sunlight into sugars and other nutrients in the chlorophyll present in its leaves. The by-product of this process is oxygen.

Potting up/on The process of putting a rooted cutting or seedling into a pot, or from a smaller pot into a larger one.

Pricking out The process of separating germinated seedlings and replanting them into a grid pattern in another container of fresh compost.

Tamp Holding the rake upright so that the tines are flat on the soil and stamping it up and down to firm up the surface after sowing.

Tilth Soil that has been raked to resemble breadcrumbs ready for sowing.

True leaves The first pair of leaves that resemble the leaves of the plant. They emerge after the rounded seed leaves.

Tuber Swollen roots that have formed storage organs, such as potatoes.

Volunteer A useful Americanism that translates as self-sown seedlings: weeds or otherwise.

Index